LOOKING BEFORE WE LEAP: SOCIAL SCIENCE AND WELFARE REFORM

edited by
R. Kent Weaver and William Dickens
The Brookings Institution

Rebecca Blank, *Northwestern University*
Evelyn Z. Brodkin, *University of Chicago*
Gary Burtless, *The Brookings Institution*
Lawrence Jacobs, *University of Minnesota*
LaDonna Pavetti, *The Urban Institute*
Robert Reischauer, *The Brookings Institution*
Mark Rom, *Georgetown University*
Robert Y. Shapiro, *Columbia University*

August 1995

Foreword

Welfare reform was one of the central elements of the House Republican leadership's Contract with America. After quick passage of a legislative package by the Republican majority in the House of Representatives in the spring of 1995, welfare reform bogged down in the Senate. Welfare promises to be one of the most important and most contentious issues confronted by Congress and the Clinton administration in the period leading up to the 1996 election. And the outcome of the welfare debate clearly has major implications for the more than four million American families who rely on the Aid to Families with Dependent Children program for part or all of their cash income.

The welfare reform debate has been loud and hard-fought, but political and budgetary calculations have often drowned out evidence about what is and is not likely to work in addressing the problems of poverty and dependence among low-income families. This new Brookings occasional paper, *Looking Before We Leap: Social Science and Welfare Reform*, is intended to help fill this gap. In this study, the contributors address what is known about such issues as the impact of converting the AFDC program into a block grant, the probable consequences of so-called "conservative mandates" such as family caps and teen mother exclusions, and the potential for moving poor single-parent families from welfare to work. They also suggest a number of specific legislative steps that could be taken to improve programs to help poor families.

The editors wish to thank Sharon Hoke, Stephanianna Lozito, Theodore Noell and Neil Siegel for research assistance; Cindy Terrels for preparing the document for publication; and Nancy Davidson and James Schneider for editing the manuscript. The Brookings Institution is grateful to the Annie E. Casey Foundation for a grant to support the research, writing, and publication of this volume.

The views expressed in his volume are solely those of the contributors and should not be ascribed to the persons whose assistance is acknowledged, to the source of funding support, or to the trustees, officers, or staff members of the Brookings Institution.

Bruce K. MacLaury
President

August 1995
Washington, D.C.

Contents

1. Looking Before We Leap: An Introduction

R. Kent Weaver and William T. Dickens

Congress is currently considering unprecedented changes in income transfer and health programs that aid the poorest Americans — the group of programs that has come to be known as "welfare." Reforms proposed by congressional Republicans would make especially important changes in programs for poor families. These reforms would remove the entitlement status of the Aid to Families with Dependent Children (AFDC) program, converting it into a block grant and essentially freezing federal expenditures at fiscal year 1994 levels for five years. Thus the real value of federal expenditures would decline. Many federal mandates to the states would be ended, and the states would not be required to maintain their existing spending levels in order to get federal block grant funds.

Proposed reforms would also dramatically increase the requirements that states move recipients from welfare to work and would place a limit of five years (consecutive or nonconsecutive) on the amount of time that an individual could receive services financed by the family assistance block grant. The House-passed bill prohibits the use of federal block grant funds for cash benefits to unmarried teenage mothers, for additional benefits to women who conceive children while receiving AFDC, and for benefits to most legal immigrants.

Critics of these proposals, including members of the Clinton administration, have charged that they would strengthen incentives for states to reduce their own spending on poor families, creating a "race to the bottom" in which states try to export their welfare recipients to other states by increasing the stinginess of their own policies. But the Clinton administration has also responded to Republican pressures by moving somewhat to the right on welfare since its 1994 welfare proposal, endorsing "hard time limits" (a period after which individuals would not receive either cash benefits or employment in the form of community service or subsidized jobs). The administration has also acted recently to expedite the waiver process for states that wish to undertake initiatives in a number of specific areas. An effort by Senate Majority Leader Robert Dole to push a compromise bill (S. 1120) through the Senate in August 1995 collapsed. The bill was opposed by both conservative Republicans, who wanted stronger provisions to reduce teenage pregnancies and tougher work requirements, and Senate Democrats, who sought to preserve state maintenance of effort and conditional entitlement for recipients who follow program rules in working toward self sufficiency. Conflict over the distribution of funds also contributed to the demise of the Dole plan. Nonetheless, welfare reform promises to be one of the most important issues confronting Congress in the fall of 1995.

Social Science and Welfare Reform

Policy change of the enormous scope contemplated by all of the welfare reform proposals currently on the agenda is inevitably a leap into the unknown. It requires projections about how state and local governments will implement the new policies and how recipients themselves will respond. What is the role of social science in such a situation? How can it act as a guide for policy? And what lessons can and should policymakers draw?

The argument of this volume is threefold. First, social science, particularly evaluations conducted of past welfare reform experiments, can provide important insights regarding the promise, limitations, and risks associated with many of the welfare reform proposals currently on the policy agenda. We believe it is important, as the title of this volume suggests, that federal policymakers look at available evidence before leaping into untested welfare reforms.

Second, we believe that whenever possible, the *degree* as well as the direction of innovation in welfare policies should be guided by the information that social science provides. Where it is clear that proposed reforms will have positive effects, it makes sense for the federal government to mandate that all states adopt those reforms. Where there is less certainty and more risk of harm to the most vulnerable families, policymakers should proceed more cautiously. States should be encouraged to experiment with state options (requiring no federal waiver) where the risks are low and federal waivers where the risks are more serious. Where the risks of specific policy innovations clearly outweigh their potential benefits, the federal government should prohibit states from making changes. (The following chapter on block grants includes a more detailed discussion of these principles.)

Third, we believe that as welfare reforms are adopted and implemented, care must be taken to ensure that these reforms are evaluated carefully so that future policymaking can be informed by their record. Policy innovation should be designed to ensure that it can be evaluated, and federal legislation should mandate evaluations and provide adequate resources to carry them out.

Unfortunately, as the chapters that follow show, none of these "looking before we leap" principles are being heeded in the current debate. Instead of basing proposals for reform on a careful weighing of existing social science evidence about welfare recipients and what is needed to move them toward self-sufficiency and meet the needs of their children, the current round of welfare reform has been driven primarily by political competition, deficit reduction pressures, and wishful thinking about the behavioral effects of policy change.

The lack of a firm evidentiary base for bold policy action is particularly true of the so-called conservative mandates: family caps, teenage mother exclusions, and hard time limits. As chapter 3 shows, evidence on whether these mandates will achieve their desired purposes exists only for the family cap issue, and that evidence is both very preliminary and very mixed. As chapter 4 shows, there is ample evidence from past experience in administering welfare programs suggesting that states will have trouble moving recipients from welfare to work as quickly and completely as pending legislative proposals require, especially in big cities. Moreover, states may respond to altered incentives by simply cutting recipients off the rolls. This evidence has been ignored in the current debate as all parties have competed to appear "tough on work."

The second "looking before we leap" principle — tailoring the degree of change to the level of knowledge and risk — is also being ignored by many actors in this round of welfare reform. Again, this is particularly true of the conservative mandates. Given the very serious risks that teenage mother exclusions and hard time limits pose for poor children, and the limited knowledge available about whether they will achieve their desired effects, national mandates for such policies would be irresponsible. State experimentation under federal guidelines is a much more prudent policy choice.

The third "looking before we leap" principle, that future reforms should be carefully monitored, is also at risk in the current round of welfare. Both the House-passed bill and the bill introduced by Senator Dole sensibly provide an additional $10 million a year for fiscal years 1996-2000 to expand the Survey of Income and Program Participation to evaluate the effects of current initiatives.[1] But it remains to be seen whether even this limited source of information can be protected from future budget-cutting initiatives. Moreover, as chapter 2 suggests, there are questions about whether unregulated state experimentation can produce evidence that will be very helpful to policymakers. Even if this round of welfare reform succeeds in "ending welfare as we know it," it almost certainly will not be the last round of welfare reform. It is essential to preserve and enhance the capacity to evaluate these critical policy changes.

The five chapters that follow examine a number of lessons about the constraints on and potential for welfare reform. Chapter 2 concentrates on financing arrangements for family assistance programs and in particular on the implications of block grants. Chapter 3 provides a "welfare primer" in a question-and-answer format, focusing on specific problems of the welfare system (such as out-of-wedlock births and difficulties in finding and retaining employment for welfare mothers) and current proposals for addressing those problems. Chapter 4 addresses the problems of implementing welfare programs, examining state capacity to assume a larger welfare role. Chapter 5 analyzes the politics of welfare reform in historical perspective, focusing on the policymaking traps that have frustrated past reform efforts. Chapter 6 examines the recent evolution of public opinion on welfare issues and the extent to which public opinion has coalesced around any particular set of proposals.

Policy Recommendations

The "look before we leap" principles suggest a number of specific policy recommendations for this round of welfare reform. We do not attempt here to develop a comprehensive plan for welfare reform, a task that is best left to legislative and executive policymakers. Instead, we focus on a few of the key issues that Congress and the president will be facing as they debate welfare reform in the fall of 1995.

Entitlements versus Block Grants

The current AFDC program is an entitlement guaranteeing eligibility to families that meet income and asset limits. Federal spending thus fluctuates with the economy. Both the House-passed welfare reform bill and S. 1120, the welfare reform bill introduced by Senator Dole, would convert AFDC and related programs into largely fixed-sum block grants. (There are modest sums provided in both bills for increased funding for states with high population growth.) Neither bill would require the states to maintain their current level of welfare spending in order to receive federal funding, but both bills contain penalties for states that fail to meet work participation rate requirements.

Chapter 2 of this volume argues that block grants have many potential shortcomings as a vehicle for delivering assistance to poor families. While they may produce policy innovation, they are less likely to produce the systematic evaluations needed so that other states can learn from pioneering states' experiences. Moreover, because they dramatically increase the incentives for states to reduce their own spending on family assistance payments, they are likely to contribute to a "race to the bottom" in aid to poor families. Block grants are also likely to freeze in place a funding formula that provides insufficient funds to poor states while shifting almost all of the uncertainty about fluctuations in caseloads to the states. A more responsible set of reforms would include the following:

- Retain the existing system of family assistance payments as an entitlement to the states, but create an expedited waiver authority and expand state options to act without waivers in some areas (for example, family caps).

- Create federal "challenge grants" that will bear an increased share of the costs of state-level experiments.

- If welfare spending cuts must be made to meet budget reduction objectives, consider reducing federal matching rates on family assistance payments above some level, thus requiring states where benefits are high to bear more of the cost of benefits.

- If Congress does adopt block grants for AFDC and related programs, it should (1) include state maintenance-of-effort requirements, (2) include a formula to provide additional grant funds in case of economic downturns, (3) change the distribution formula among states over time to reflect the number of poor children in a state rather than past spending practices, and (4) exclude conservative mandates for teenage mother exclusions and hard time limits.

- Even if AFDC and related programs are converted into a block grant, the Food Stamp program should be retained as a federal entitlement. However, an expedited waiver process should be established that would allow state experiments to use pooled family assistance payments and Food Stamp funds for welfare-to-work demonstrations.

Family Caps

Proposals to prohibit the payment of additional family assistance benefits to mothers who conceive children while receiving AFDC have been among the most controversial elements in this round of welfare reform. Proponents argue that a family cap will change the behavior of recipients, reducing additional births to this group; critics charge that it will simply make poor children worse off without having a significant impact on out-of-wedlock births, or that it will increase abortions. The Clinton administration's 1994 welfare proposal and Senator Dole's bill both allowed family caps as a state option, while the House-passed welfare bill prohibits the use of federal funds for such payments. As noted in chapter 3, existing evidence from New Jersey is both very preliminary in nature and quite mixed in its conclusions. The early state of research on family caps suggests the following recommendations:

- States should be allowed to experiment with family caps for family assistance payments as a state option without requiring a federal waiver. However, states should not be compelled to adopt them either for their own funds or for federal funds. If Congress does mandate family caps, states should be allowed to opt out of the caps by passing a statute exempting themselves from the mandate. Alternatively, implementation of the mandate could be delayed for five years until better results are available from the state-level experiments.

- Because Food Stamp benefits also increase with family size and decline as cash income (including AFDC benefits) rises, the Food Stamp program undercuts some of the effect of a family cap in family assistance payments. To test the importance of this effect, some states should be granted waivers to impose a family cap on Food Stamp benefits as well as family assistance payments.

- The family cap approach should not be used in the Medicaid program; additional children born to mothers receiving family assistance payments should continue to be eligible for Medicaid.

Teenage Mother Exclusions

Like family caps, excluding teenage mothers from eligibility for family assistance payments has been advocated as an effective mechanism for reducing out-of-wedlock births among the group that is most likely to end up as long-term AFDC recipients. Critics charge that such an exclusion will hurt poor children and increase burdens on an already severely strained foster care system but will have little impact on births to teenage parents. The House-passed welfare bill prohibits use of federal funds to pay cash benefits to teenage mothers but allows states to provide vouchers for certain necessary commodities and permits those mothers to become eligible for cash payments when they reach age 18. Senator Dole's bill allows teenage mother exclusions as a state option; the Clinton administration's 1994 welfare reform proposal required teenage mothers to live in an adult-supervised environment in most circumstances, but preserved their eligibility for cash benefits.

There is virtually no direct evidence on the effects of teenage mother exclusions. Moreover, acquiring such evidence through the usual technique of random assignment to treatment and control groups is not likely to provide an adequate test of the potential of such a policy to reduce teenage pregnancies, since it requires a change in community-wide expectations about the assistance available to pregnant teenagers. Given the potential for serious harm to children from teenage mother exclusions, and the lack of evidence, the most reasonable course of action is as follows:

- States should neither be mandated nor given the unrestricted option to enact teenage mother exclusions.

- If the state-level family cap experiments appear to show promising results in reducing pregnancies among AFDC mothers, the federal government should consider allowing one or a very few metropolitan areas to experiment under federal waivers with excluding teenage mothers from cash benefits. Care must be taken in these experiments to meet the increased needs at child welfare agencies.

• If a teenage mother exclusion experiment is undertaken in some states or cities, other regions and states should be required to apply the rules of the state of origin to teenage mothers in order to prevent migration that would interfere with the effects of the experiments. Federal challenge grant funds should be provided for an intensive evaluation of these experiments.

Work Requirements, Work Support, and Participation Requirements

Proposals to increase work requirements for welfare recipients have been a prominent feature of all major welfare reform proposals in the current round, reflecting their very broad popularity with the public (see the discussion in chapter 6). Work requirements raise several important issues. Which parents should be required to work? What activities should reasonably be counted as "work"? What supportive services (e.g. child care, transportation) should be provided to those persons subject to a work requirement? And what work participation targets should the states be required to meet? All of these are difficult policy choices, and there are no simple "right" answers. But the principles outlined earlier in this chapter do provide a helpful measuring stick for judging current legislative proposals — and they do not measure up well.

The first two principles are that (1) policy change should be based on a careful evaluation of past experience and state administrative and financial capacity, and (2) the degree as well as the direction of policy change should reflect what we know from past experience; where we know less, caution should take precedence over boldness. Unfortunately, current legislative proposals pay inadequate attention to what we know about what is required to move low-skilled mothers from welfare to work and how successful they are likely to be in staying off of welfare. Mothers of young children can not be expected to work or look for work unless they are provided with child care. Given the poor preparation for work of most welfare recipients, an extended job search of many months will be common. Even once employed, women earning the minimum wage will find child care prohibitively expensive. If they are to continue to work many will need state provided or subsidized child care. Many mothers will eventually earn more than the minimum wage, but given the lack of job preparation typical of long-term welfare mothers, low wages in entry level jobs are to be expected. Further, low wage employment tends to be very unstable. Welfare mothers will find themselves facing repeated spells of unemployment.

Experience also shows that effective welfare-to-work programs require the provision of additional services. It is not enough to tell a high school drop-out with no job experience who grew up in a family where no one worked to go out and get a job. At a minimum, such women need help in obtaining the basic skills of job search, and counselling on what employers expect from their workers in the way of attendance, respect, and reliability. Further, the most effective welfare-to-work programs go beyond counselling and act as job brokers. Such programs require unusually devoted staff with high morale, and quality staff are not cheap. Finally, the cost effectiveness of programs which provide extended training or education are dubious, but such programs provide the most realistic hope of significantly increasing the income of large numbers of welfare families so that they can be permanently lifted from dependence.

Even the most effective welfare-to-work programs are able to achieve only small improvements in the employment rates of welfare recipients. It is possible that tough work requirements with rigid time limits will induce greater work effort on the part of welfare recipients, but it is at least as likely that the expectations on which those requirements are based are unrealistic. Single mothers with little job preparation face tremendous obstacles to becoming and then staying employed. The consequences of unrealistic expectations could be catastrophic — homeless families, and children separated from their mothers and institutionalized. *We have no experience with tough work requirements for women with children and have no idea what their effects will be.*

The problems with proposals for work requirements for individuals are exacerbated by current proposals for state work participation rates. In both Republican and Democratic bills, these provisions have been influenced not by past state experience with what is achievable but rather by a desire not to be portrayed by the other political party as "weak on work." Senator Dole's bill, for example, mandates 50 percent participation rates in work activities by the year 2000; the same participation rate is required by the year 2003 in the House-passed bill. The Senate Democratic alternative introduced by Minority Leader Daschle (S. 1117) also mandates a 50 percent "work performance rate" by the year 2000. For two-parent families, the required participation rates reach 90 percent in FY 1998 in the House bill and in 1999 in Senator Dole's bill. All of these participation rates are far higher than the highest participation rate ever achieved by any state to date. Moreover, while both the House bill and Senator Dole's welfare reform bills expect the states to do much more to put recipients to work, they provide states with fewer resources to accomplish the task. Achieving higher participation rates will require more resources because putting welfare recipients to work is expensive. Requiring states to increase their participation rates without giving them adequate resources to do so is simply a gigantic unfunded mandate to the states.

One way to make work requirements for large numbers of recipients realistic would be for the state to act as an employer of last resort. As paradoxical as it may seem, it is much more expensive for a state to provide jobs than welfare. The development of public service jobs or workfare requires additional administrative capacity and careful supervision of the workfare employees to ensure attendance and work effort. Rarely is it practical to replace existing state workers with workfare employees so it is not possible to recoup the cost of the program from savings elsewhere.

As discussed in chapter 4, the combination of increased federal requirements and decreased support from the federal government puts states in a triple bind. If states attempt to hold spending constant while expanding the size of their welfare-to-work programs, the quality of their programs will suffer. If they ignore participation requirements, they face federal fiscal penalties, further decreasing their capacity to promote transitions from welfare to work. This means either increasing their own expenditures or cutting welfare benefits. Few are likely to choose the former. However, if states adopt benefit cuts sufficient to fund work programs, they will reduce the well-being of the very families they are trying to help. Moreover, this would be a very risky course since no program has ever demonstrated the ability to achieve the participation rates mandated by existing legislation. More likely, states will react to federal mandates for increased work by attempting to reduce welfare participation — particularly by those who will have the hardest time finding work. Such behavior could exacerbate the "race-to-the-bottom" as families denied benefits or harassed off AFDC in one state flee to others in the hope of finding more lenient administrations.

A third principle that should guide welfare reform is the preservation of capacity to learn from experimentation. Current legislative proposals do not provide adequately for evaluating the experiences of the states as they make use of their new freedom and new flexibility. As discussed in chapter 2, evaluations are a collective good for which individual states incur significant added costs and from which they reap only limited benefits — and state politicians may reap no benefits at all. It is thus especially important that the federal government underwrite the costs of evaluations.

Based on these considerations, welfare reform legislation should contain the following elements:

- The federal government should set work participation requirements that are consistent with the amount of federal funding provided and that do not provide incentives to push recipients off of welfare through inappropriate use of sanctions or churning them in and out of temporary jobs. If federal funding is frozen at 1994 levels, participation rate requirements should also be frozen at those levels. If Congress does not increase funding for work, it should eliminate financial penalties to the states for not meeting those targets.

- Work participation requirements for states should not provide incentives to states to improve their rating by cutting recipients off without providing them access to employment.

- Individuals should never be sanctioned for failing to work unless there are jobs available to them. Federal legislation should guarantee this right for the sake of children.

- Welfare recipients should not be required to participate in work activities unless they have access to affordable child care. States should be permitted to exempt from work requirements parents for whom child care is not available.

- State effort on work activities that increases net state expenditures above FY 1995 levels should be rewarded with a 50 percent federal match.

- States should be permitted to exempt mothers of children under age 1 from calculation of work participation rates.

- The federal government should provide a pool of "challenge grant" funds, providing up to a 60 percent match in funds for the costs of testing promising state experiments in moving welfare recipients from welfare to work and up to 80 percent for evaluation of those experiments. Federal administrative capacity to facilitate such evaluations and disseminate their results should be augmented, not eliminated.

Hard Time Limits

Hard time limits have a number of parallels to teenage mother exclusions: (1) their effects are complex; (2) the potential risks to the welfare of children are great; (3) there is virtually no direct evidence on how they would alter the behavior of present and potential welfare recipients; and (4) classic control and treatment group methodologies for evaluating program effects are poor vehicles for testing their effects, because the success of the policy change depends on changing expectations in the community at large. However, the potentially very high costs of hard time limits for poor children, and evidence from current welfare caseloads suggesting that many women will not be able to find and retain steady employment in the private sector, suggest taking a fairly cautious course:

- Hard time limits should not be implemented as a nationwide policy or as an unlimited state option. Experiments may be desirable under federal waivers, if states agree to detailed, federally financed evaluations.

- It is especially important that states not be allowed to set hard time limits at whatever duration they choose. If hard time limits are legislated, a federal minimum is needed. Allowing unlimited state discretion on hard time limits is likely to set off a particularly ferocious "race to the bottom" in which states will seek to avoid becoming a "welfare magnet" for recipients from low benefit-duration states. Until more is understood about how the current round of reforms will affect welfare caseloads and whether the reforms will allow women in single-parent families to avoid repeated cycling through the welfare system, any federal minimum should be set at no less than five years.

- If Congress decides to adopt hard time limits, it is imperative that there be sufficient exemptions to prevent undue hardship to children whose mothers turn out not to be employable. Until more is known about how other aspects of welfare reform will affect the employment prospects of these mothers, it is preferable to err on the side of caution. Exemption levels, if enacted, should be set at no less than twenty percent of the caseload.

- To avoid the problem of denying eligibility to women who manage to stay off welfare for an extended period but then suffer a job loss or marital breakup, any hard time limit should include provisions allowing former recipients to "earn back" limited eligibility — for example, one month of eligibility for each 6 months off the rolls, up to a total of a year of renewed eligibility.

The Prospects for Welfare Reform

Is a comprehensive welfare reform package likely to emerge from Congress this year? What sort of a package is most likely to be enacted into law? Insights from past welfare reform initiatives and from public opinion can help to answer these questions. They are discussed in the last two chapters of this volume. The evidence from past rounds of welfare reform, summarized in chapter 5, suggests that the obstacles facing any comprehensive welfare reform initiative are formidable. Thus the conservative Republican strategy of pushing for maximum simultaneous change on a variety of fronts is a risky one. Past efforts to produce radical change in the system generally ended in stalemate. Incremental change, while still difficult, is more likely to succeed. Whether it will be possible to build a successful legislative coalition in the present polarized environment remains very much in doubt, even if the budget reconciliation bill is used as a vehicle.

Public opinion evidence, discussed in chapter 6, suggests that the public is fairly cautious in its attitudes toward welfare reform. The current welfare system is widely despised and seen as needing radical reform. But the public retains a substantial concern about the fate of poor children and policy initiatives that might put them at risk. There is overwhelming support for work requirements, child care funding, and job training, but substantial ambivalence on most other issues, depending on whether questions primarily tap concerns about (unpopular) parents or (popular) children. While recent polls have shown the public thinks congressional Republicans have better ideas for welfare reform than President Clinton, opinion has been highly volatile. Welfare reform is an issue that poses dangers for both political parties because it can reinforce negative images that the public has of each party: that the Democrats tolerate irresponsible behavior by the poor and that the Republicans want to take money away from the helpless and give it to the rich.

The current round of welfare reform may produce unprecedented change in a direction that the public supports, toward a system that gives increased emphasis to work and self-sufficiency. But budgetary pressures and political competition have also pushed welfare reform in directions that pose unprecedented risks. On the one hand, there are risks that a faulty funding mechanism, unattainable work requirements, and untested mandates to alter the behavior of the poor may lead to a social disaster for America's most vulnerable citizens. On the other hand, there is also the risk that the same problems will lead to a political stalemate that will not solve the problems of America's poor and will further alienate the American public. Both of these extremes must be avoided.

2. Financing Welfare: Are Block Grants the Answer?

Robert D. Reischauer and R. Kent Weaver

The welfare reform bill passed by the House of Representatives in March 1995 and the bill sponsored by Senate Majority Leader Robert Dole both make unprecedented changes in financing the Aid to Families with Dependent Children (AFDC) program and a number of other programs that provide cash aid, nutritional assistance, and social services to low-income citizens. Both bills would convert AFDC from an open-ended, matching grant program into an essentially fixed-sum block grant to the states. For at least the first five years, the size of the block grant received by each state would be determined by the amount of its 1994 federal funding.[2]

This chapter examines the appropriateness of block grants for delivering assistance to low-income families. At first glance, the advantages seem considerable. For the states, block grants hold out the promise of reduced federal regulation and a chance to use Washington's money to pay for state-designed programs that may be better tailored than federal programs to local values and conditions. For the federal government, block grants promise a limit on federal exposure to increasing expenditures on means-tested programs, especially in the rapidly-growing Medicaid program. The details of the incentive structure that block grants would create, however, make it clear that they have serious shortcomings.

In thinking about how welfare reform bills should be changed to overcome these shortcomings, it is useful to consider four objectives that federal financing and standard-setting mechanisms should accomplish in a system in which the federal government and the states share program responsibility. First, they should promote policy innovation and evaluation by the states. Second, a federal financing and standard-setting system should prevent a race to the bottom, pernicious competition in which the states reduce benefits and eligibility in an effort to reduce inmigration and promote outmigration by present and potential welfare recipients. Third, a federal financing and standard-setting mechanism should distribute funds equitably among states and individuals. Finally, it should also distribute risks — notably the risk of economic downturns — equitably among levels of government. On each of these criteria, the block grant bills being considered in Congress have serious deficiencies.

This chapter first reviews the ways in which the federal government can structure the financing and standard setting of shared-cost programs. It then discusses the extent to which the House-passed and Senate welfare reform bills meet each of the four objectives and suggests improvements that should be made in them. Our focus is on the bills' AFDC provisions, although many of the same arguments could be extended to Food Stamps and other programs. Rather than suggesting a single best set of modifications to address the bills' shortcomings, we will present two packages of policy options. Option A retains the block grant structure of the congressional proposals, but makes specific improvements over current proposals in Congress. Option B builds on the current system of individual entitlements, but also makes specific improvements. These options are summarized in table 2-1.

Table 2-1. Policy Options for Welfare Program Reform

Policy objective	Option A (block-grant based)	Option B (entitlement-based)
Promote innovation and evaluation	Remove conservative mandates, allow states to opt out of them, or delay their implementation until rigorous state experiments can be conducted	Create expedited waiver process, allowing entire states to serve as experiment sites with increased Survey on Income and Program Participation funding to allow evaluation of these experiments
		Create federal challenge grants for promising state experiments and evaluation
Prevent a race to the bottom	Require state maintenance of effort on a per capita basis	Use waiver process to minimize race to the bottom
Distribute funds equitably to states and individuals	Change distribution of block grant over time to reflect changes in population of poor children	Cap federal match on state benefit levels or reduce federal match on high benefits
Share the risk of economic downturns	Vary amount of block grant with economic conditions in the state or increase size of "Rainy Day Fund" and convert it into a grant	

Financing and Standard-Setting Options in a Federal System

Two critical aspects of any program in which responsibility is shared between the federal and state governments are the nature of the federal transfer to the states and the restrictiveness of the standards that states need to meet to obtain federal funds without incurring penalties.

Financing alternatives in shared federal-state programs differ in two ways: the requirements they impose on states to match federal funds and the extent to which states' actions can increase or decrease the amounts received from the federal government. *Block grants*, which are at one extreme, generally distribute a fixed sum of money to the states according to a formula; some grants allow states to choose from among several formulas the one that is most advantageous to them. Block grants do not impose any requirement that the states match federal funds. They can usually be used for broad purposes with a minimum of federal restrictions. When the funds must be used for narrow purposes and possibly require some state matching funds, they are called *categorical grants. Open-ended matching grants*, such as the AFDC and Medicaid programs, are near the other end of the spectrum. They require the states to match federal expenditures, although the matching rate can vary (as it does in both AFDC and Medicaid), generally according to a state's fiscal capacity. *Capped matching grants* use a formula to distribute funds among the states, but set a ceiling on the funds available to individual states or to all states collectively or both. *Demonstration or challenge grants* give still more discretion to the federal government: state governments submit proposals and the federal government chooses the projects that seem to be most promising. In other words, no state can be assured it will receive federal funds.

Shared federal-state programs also vary in the extent to which the federal government sets standards (for example, eligibility and benefit standards in income transfer programs). Among the potential options are the following, listed in order from those allowing states the least discretion to those allowing the most.

—*Uniform federal standards*, which allow no state discretion. All states, for example, are required to use uniform eligibility and benefit standards in administering the Food Stamp program.

—*Uniform federal standards with waiver provisions*, used by a few programs, allow state governments to apply to the federal government for waivers in federal program provisions. More than half the states currently have AFDC waivers from the Department of Health and Human Services under which they are testing ideas such as family caps (no additional benefits for children conceived or born while a mother is receiving AFDC), and "learnfare" (penalties for teenage AFDC mothers who do not meet school attendance objectives and rewards for those who do).

—*Uniform federal standards with state options* offer states opt-out or opt-in alternatives. In the Medicaid program, for example, states are offered the option to cover some services (eyeglasses and prescription drugs, for example) with federal reimbursement in addition to a mandatory package of services. States can also cover groups in addition to the ones they must cover, which include recipients of Supplemental Security Income, AFDC recipients, and certain low-income children and pregnant women.[3]

—Rather than requiring a state to get approval for any deviation from federal standards, the federal government can also set a range of acceptable values within which the states can choose: *federal minimum and maximum values*. States can, for example, be required to offer Medicaid coverage to persons below a certain income level and forbidden to offer coverage to persons above a higher level, but allowed discretion in whether they will cover persons at intermediate levels.

—Finally, the federal government can impose no standards at all on the states, or standards that are essentially meaningless. This is the case with benefit levels in the current AFDC program because states set their own need standards on which AFDC payments are based.

The standard-setting and financing provisions in federal-state programs are usually linked: matching grants are more likely than block grants to have detailed and strict federal requirements attached. In the case of current welfare reform legislation, however, the block grants in the House-passed bill are restrictive. The bill specifies a number of categories of persons on whom federal dollars cannot be spent, although it does allow the states to spend their own dollars on them. Neither the House nor the Senate bill requires the states to maintain their current levels of funding to qualify for this aid, but both have stiffer requirements than those in the current AFDC program for states to move welfare recipients into work activities. In addition, the House bill contains new "conservative mandates" restricting the payment of cash benefits to teenage mothers and increases in payments when a mother conceives and bears a child while receiving benefits from AFDC or its successor program. Both bills limit to five years the use of federal funds for cash or work-related benefits provided to those receiving family assistance.

Promoting Innovation and Evaluation

One potential advantage of using block grants to aid poor families is that states' discretion could be increased, which might encourage experimentation and lead eventually to better policies. Experimentation is desirable because current programs are not working well, and analysts are unsure of what changes might improve them. Once policies have been tried in a few pathbreaking states, other states might emulate them, and perhaps the federal government would eventually take over or standardize policy or both if the new programs seemed successful. Because not all innovations would represent an improvement over the present system, another advantage of increased state discretion is that it would lower the costs of testing approaches that are ultimately deemed unacceptable by allowing experiments in only one or two states rather than nationwide.

Experimentation at the state level can be particularly useful when new policy ideas are thought to have both beneficial and harmful consequences, but the relative magnitudes of the effects are unknown. For example, as noted in chapter 3 of this book, it is likely that hard time limits, limits after which recipients would not be granted further cash benefits nor guaranteed jobs, would increase employment among welfare recipients but would also increase hardship and homelessness. The relative magnitudes of the effects are not clear because time limits of this type have never been tested.

The desirability of these policy experiments does not mean that states should have unlimited discretion to test policy alternatives, however. Experiments should be designed to produce reliable information that helps answer important questions. In particular, results must be carefully evaluated and variations in a policy that may be important to its success or failure must be tested.

Using waivers has the advantage of allowing the federal government to ensure that a variety of approaches are tried, that careful evaluations are done, and that approaches that seem likely to have significant harmful consequences are avoided.[4] Of course, a waiver process is also likely to delay state-based innovation compared with the time it would take in a more permissive system. Moreover, waivers that require policy innovations to be cost-neutral to the federal government (as is the case with the current AFDC waiver system) are likely to limit experiments to those that pose few costs and financial risks for the states. Encouraging innovation by using waivers is likely to be most successful when combined with challenge grants that compel the federal government to share in the risk of policy experiments by sharing the costs.

Although states should have the flexibility to try out some policy variations, other deviations from federal standards should have to be approved by the federal government through waivers. But where should states be given wide latitude, and where should that freedom be circumscribed by waiver requirements? A sensible principle is that the mechanisms used to set program standards should take account of both the anticipated consequences of an experiment and the conditions needed to gain usable knowledge from it. Welfare reform should move forward boldly, with uniform national mandates, when we can be reasonably certain the consequences of innovation will be beneficial. If probable costs of state discretion are low and potential benefits are significant, but the magnitude of those benefits or the exact combination of standards needed to maximize them is uncertain, the federal government may wish not only to allow state discretion but to encourage it — for example, by funding all the costs of a state experiment through a challenge grant. If the potential costs of broad discretion are low and the advantages are uncertain, states should be given wide latitude in policymaking, with few federal controls. But the federal government should move more cautiously, using waivers or minimum and maximum standards, when costs or beneficial outcomes are less certain, and more cautiously still when the potential costs of innovation seem very high. If the likely costs of state discretion are high and the advantages few — if discretion is certain to provoke a "race to the bottom," for example — it should be prohibited and uniform national standards should be imposed.

The bill passed by the House and the one sponsored by Majority Leader Dole in the Senate violate these principles in three ways. First, they are likely to provide insufficient encouragement to state experiments that cost more money (at least in the short run) because the state government will bear the entire burden of increased costs. Experiments that do occur are likely to be biased in the direction of those that produce short-term cost reduction, (e.g., various time limits).

A second problem with current bills is that even if they result in a proliferation of policy innovation, they are likely to produce insufficient evaluation. Careful evaluations may not be in the interests of local politicians, who may have a greater interest in claiming success for successful program innovations than running a well-designed and implemented random assignment trial-- especially when the state is bearing 100 percent of the costs of that evaluation and will not gain all of the "learning" benefits. It is likely that block grants will produce numerous-- and loud-- claims by governors about the success of their states in cutting caseloads and moving workers from welfare to work, but little in the way of useful evaluations that will allow us to judge those claims.

Third, while both the House and Senate bills provide a great deal of flexibility to states in some aspects of program design, they also impose some new nationwide requirements despite the fact that there is little knowledge about the possible effects of those requirements. Both bills, for example, would impose hard limits on the duration of benefits, and the House bill would mandate caps on family size and preclude cash payments to teenage mothers. Hard time limits could lead to a significant increase in employment among AFDC parents or they could produce widespread homelessness and hardship if many recipients lacked the skills needed to compete successfully in job markets. Similarly, the exclusion of teenage mothers and the imposition of family caps could reduce births or have no effect on births and increase hardship for children of teenage mothers and those in families with an additional birth.

If Congress adopts block grant welfare, it should do so without the untested and potentially very harmful conservative mandates in the House bill. Not only are these mandates questionable on their own merits, they also risk increased federal mandates and set-asides within the family assistance block grant, repeating a pattern of ever greater federal intrusion that has characterized other block grant programs.[5]

At an absolute minimum, Congress should allow a state to choose to ignore conservative mandates whose effects are unknown if its legislature and governor agree. Alternatively, the effective date of these mandates could be delayed for five years so that rigorous experiments could be conducted in several states to estimate the effect of each mandate. The results of such experiments are likely to provide a mixed answer. For example, time limits may lead to both more employment and more hardship. But policymakers will still have a better understanding of the trade-offs. Even if employment were not increased, policymakers could decide the mandate is desirable because it would restore public confidence in the program or reaffirm society's values.

The more cautious and humane path to welfare reform would involve maintaining the existing entitlement nature of AFDC while supporting innovation and experimentation. Congress should create an expedited waiver process, allowing entire states to serve as experiment sites with increased funding from the Survey on Income and Program Participation for evaluation of the experiments. Congress should also create federal challenge grants to help bear the costs of promising state experiments and evaluation.

Preventing a Race to the Bottom

Perhaps the most serious risk associated with the block grants for welfare is that the reform may stimulate states to restrict welfare eligibility and reduce benefits in order to be less attractive to present and potential welfare recipients. As noted in chapter 3 of this volume, it is not necessary that there actually *be* powerful migration effects to set off a competitive race to the bottom in benefits; it is enough that policymakers *perceive* that such effects exist.

States can set off interstate competition by tightening eligibility and benefit standards for social programs and, when Congress and the courts allow it, establishing residency requirements for receipt of benefits.[6] A more subtle or passive form that the race to the bottom can take is to let inflation erode the value of benefits, which are set in nominal dollar terms. After the early 1970s, most states failed to adjust AFDC benefits fully for inflation. Real benefits for a family of four with no other income fell by 47 percent in the median state between 1970 and 1993, a decline that was only partially compensated by increases in Food Stamp benefits.[7] Food Stamp and federal Supplemental Security Income benefits, which are both indexed and standardized, did not undergo a similar erosion.[8]

The House and Senate welfare reform block grant proposals dramatically alter the incentives to states in ways that are likely to prompt a race to the bottom. Under the block grant structure, states will have to spend more of their own money than they do under the existing matching grant structure if they want to increase a family's combined family support and Food Stamp benefits by a certain amount.

Under the current system of matching grants, an increase in state AFDC payments results in an increase in federal matching funds — roughly dollar for dollar in high-income states and more than three-to-one in low-income states. A decrease in state payments triggers similar multiplier effects in federal funds. These effects on family income, as has been noted, are partially offset by federally funded Food Stamp benefits, which increase to partially offset a decrease in AFDC benefits and vice versa. As table 2-2 shows, under the current AFDC system, an increase of $1.00 in state spending on AFDC benefits leads to an increase in family income (AFDC benefits plus food stamps) of $1.40 in high-income states and $2.80 or more in low-income states. A decrease in state spending has the same multiplier effect. Under a block grant system, however, increased or decreased state family support payments will not trigger any change in federal family support payments, although they will be partially offset by a change in food stamp payments. In both high- and low-income states, a $1.00 increase in state payments will increase family income by only $.70. Few states will find this attractive.

They could, however, be tempted to reduce benefits. If a high-income state decided to lower its combined food stamp and family support payments by $.70 under a block grant structure, it could free up $1.00 in state funds. In short, a block grant welfare program dramatically reduces state incentives to increase spending on family support payments; indeed, it provides incentives to reduce such payments.

These same incentives will be reflected at the level of aggregate income to the states. Under the current system, an increase in state AFDC payments leads to an increase in federal AFDC matching payments that is only partially offset by falling Food Stamp benefits. The net flow of federal funds into the state increases when a state increases its effort; a high-income state with a 50 percent matching rate can expect an increase in federal funds of $.40 for every $1.00 it increases its own effort. Under a block grant, the reverse is the case; for every additional $1.00 the state devotes to AFDC, total federal aid flowing into the state will decrease by $.30. Conversely, the flow of federal aid into the state will increase by $.30 if the state cuts its effort on behalf of AFDC recipients by $1.00 (see table 2-2). In short, because federal block grant payments do not vary with state effort and Food Stamp payments vary inversely with state effort, a block grant system reverses the incentive of state governments to increase state AFDC payments to get more federal dollars flowing into the state: a greater state effort for family support payments will decrease the inflow of federal dollars. Such perverse incentives can only encourage a race to the bottom. Without the inducement of federal matching funds, state spending on poor families is likely to be squeezed out by more popular programs such as prison construction and aid to schools.

Table 2-2. Effects on Incentives to the States of Changing from Matching Grant Welfare System to Block Grant System

current dollars

Level of benefits in state	Federal matching system in effect	Change in state benefits	Effects of change in state benefits on:			
			Federal family support payments to state	Federal food stamp payments	Combined food stamp/AFDC payment to family	Inflow of federal dollars into state
Low-income state (75 percent federal match under current system)	Existing AFDC system	+1.00	+3.00	-1.20	+2.80	+1.80
	Block grant system	+1.00	0	-0.30	+0.70	-0.30
	Existing AFDC system	-1.00	-3.00	+1.20	-2.80	-1.80
	Block grant system	-1.00	0	+0.30	-0.70	+0.30
High-income state (50% federal AFDC match under current system)	Existing AFDC system	+1.00	+1.00	-0.60	+1.40	+0.40
	Block grant system	+1.00	0	-0.30	+0.70	-0.30
	Existing AFDC system	-1.00	-1.00	+0.60	-1.40	-0.40
	Block grant system	-1.00	0	+0.30	-0.70	+0.30

The dramatically reduced status of the safety net in the block grant bills is also likely to set off increased competition among states in a race to the bottom. Under the current AFDC system, states can compete to a limited degree by restricting AFDC eligibility and benefits. But the block grant proposals in Congress lack any provisions for setting a minimum period of eligibility for cash benefits or requiring states to provide jobs if individuals cannot find them in the private sector. In anticipation of this provision's becoming law, states have already begun dramatically cutting the length of time a person can receive welfare.

Block grants also increase the prospects for future reductions in family assistance expenditures at the federal level by obscuring the effects that such cuts would have on individual families. Future Congresses will certainly be tempted to cut block grant funding as they seek ways to reduce the deficit. This will be politically easier when those cuts are absorbed by fifty-one separate state programs and the repercussions on individuals are less obvious.

The net effect of this revised incentive structure is that both federal and state expenditures on poor families are likely to drop precipitously. If Congress decides to use block grants to aid poor families (option A in table 2-1), several steps should be taken to prevent a severe race to the bottom. States should be able to qualify for their current level of federal funds only if they continue existing levels of their own funding or can demonstrate progress in moving their welfare clientele not just off the welfare rolls but into employment and out of poverty. In practice, designing an adequate set of performance indicators to measure state success in increasing the self-sufficiency of welfare recipients would be difficult, however; it can be anticipated that the states would attempt to "game" any system of performance indicators to qualify for their full funding allotment.

If Congress decides to retain individual entitlement (option B in table 2-1), the federal government should not be afraid to set effective standards where there is a risk of a race to the bottom. Given the existing diversity among the states and their desire to preserve that diversity, these standards should take the form of federal minimum requirements rather than enjoin all states to have identical program standards. The federal government should also use its power to disallow waiver requests in order to ensure that state experimentation does not lead to an unravelling of the already frayed system of protections for poor children. But the federal government should allow the states to set their own policies where the risk of a race to the bottom is modest.

Distributing Funds Equitably to States and Individuals

One potential problem with any federal welfare program is that poorer states may not be able to provide levels of service to their citizens equivalent to those in richer states, or they may have to use much higher tax rates to do so.[9] For this reason federal matching grant programs such as AFDC and Medicaid include measures of state fiscal capacity and need in their formulas for federal cost sharing. However, these measures still may not fully offset the disadvantage of poorer regions because of floors or ceilings in the distribution formulas and the fact that inadequate state fiscal capacity, high levels of need, and weak public support for welfare may be correlated. This partly explains why richer regions may be able to draw down more federal dollars per capita in matching funds than poorer regions can. In 1994, for example, the nation's poorest state, Mississippi, drew only $302 per poor child in federal matching funds for AFDC, while the richest state, Connecticut, drew $1,566 per poor child. The federally funded Food Stamp program is much more effective at targeting funds at poor states than is the shared-cost AFDC program, even though AFDC has a matching formula that strongly favors poor states.

This inequitable distribution of federal funds in the AFDC program is accepted because it is a result of individual states' decisions about the amount of their resources they wish to devote to welfare. Mississippi could increase its federal AFDC payment substantially if it chose to spend more of its own money. But giving more funding per poor child to rich states than to poor states under a block grant system — simply because that was the funding system under a program that no longer exists — is indefensible. The only rationale for doing so would be to allow Congress to avoid choosing between making huge cuts in the allocations to some states or shielding states from the effects of such cuts by increasing overall expenditures on programs for poor families. Reallocating funds would be a political nightmare: if federal AFDC funding were reallocated according to the number of poor children in each state, Alaska, Hawaii, Massachusetts, Rhode Island, Vermont, and Washington would see their federal payments halved, while Alabama, Arkansas, Louisiana, Mississippi, South Carolina, and Texas would more than double their take. The likely outcome is that the winner states would use the windfall to pull out their already meager expenditures, while the loser (high-benefit) states would have to cut benefits.

The allocation mechanisms in the current House and Senate bills contain another serious flaw: they fail to take adequate account of shifts that may increase a state's population faster than the national average. These shifts will cause some states to bear an increasing share of the burden of assisting low-income families. The House bill creates an annual fund of $100 million to be divided among states with the highest rates of population growth. Senator Dole's bill provides a total of $878 million to high population growth states over five years. Neither amount is likely to be adequate.[10]

If Congress decides to adopt a block grant funding system (option A in table 2-1), an allocation mechanism more appropriate than simply freezing current funding shares needs to be developed. Indeed, a new funding formula needs to be put in place now, since experience has shown that block granting funding formulas are hard to change once they are put in place.[11] This formula should be based primarily on the number of poor children in each state. Recognizing that it will take time for states to adjust to the new fiscal realities, a ten-year transition should be put into effect: in the first year of the block grant, 10 percent of the funds would be allocated according to the number of poor children in the state and 90 percent based on the funding formula in the current House bill, with the share of funds allocated by the number of poor children increasing by 10 percent each year. It should also include a maintenance-of-effort requirement to prevent states that benefit from the formula change from getting a fiscal windfall intended to aid their children.

Retaining the current system of individual entitlements (option B) has the advantage of adjusting automatically for shifts in population among states. If Congress decides that a cap on AFDC expenditures is required, it may be desirable to consider phasing in an inflation-adjusted cap on per capita federal matches to AFDC grants, or reducing the federal match on benefits over a set amount. This would move federal resources away from the more generous (and generally more wealthy) states to those with fewer resources.

Sharing the Risks of Economic Downturn

Another important criteria for judging federal-state programs is how they share the financial risks of events that increase demand on a program. Most obviously, economic downturns decrease the number of jobs available and swell the ranks of those eligible for AFDC and Food Stamp benefits. Currently, the AFDC system plays a modest counter-cyclical role in recessions, although its effect on overall consumer spending is too modest to have much of an impact on preventing the deepening of recessions.

It is on the criterion of sharing the risk of economic downturns that the House-passed welfare reform bill makes its most important changes and is most seriously deficient. Under current law, an increase in the number of people eligible for AFDC in a state results automatically in an increase in federal matching grants to that state (federal matching rates range from 50 to roughly 80 percent) with no limit. Under both the House-passed bill and Senator Dole's welfare reform bill, however, both the overall AFDC budget and individual states' share of that budget are essentially fixed in nominal dollar terms for five years, which means that their real value will decrease. States that are hit by a recession could only *borrow* money from a "Rainy Day Fund" established by the federal government to meet the greater needs of low-income families, and they would need to repay it with interest within three years.[12] Clearly, this represents an effort to reduce the risk of unanticipated increases in federal expenditures by exporting all the costs of economic downturns to the states.

The Rainy Day Fund has been defended as analogous to the current Unemployment Insurance system in which states that have exhausted their individual trust funds for regular benefits can borrow from the federal government until the trust funds recover. Proponents of the Rainy Day Fund have also noted that Congress has repeatedly intervened to increase the duration of Unemployment Insurance benefits during recessions; a family assistance block grant might therefore expect similar treatment.

These analogies to Unemployment Insurance are deficient, however. First, the House Rainy Day Fund contains a cap of $1 billion ($1.7 billion in Senator Dole's bill); there is no such cap in the Unemployment Insurance system, and increased family assistance costs to the states can be expected to far exceed these caps in the event of a serious recession.[13] Large states, which are limited to a maximum $100 million loan from the fund, would be especially likely to come up short.[14] Second, a federal safety net for the states is already built into the Unemployment Insurance system: when unemployment rates reach legislatively defined levels, individuals who exhaust their regular benefits become eligible for extended benefits, half the cost of which is financed by the federal government, with no repayment by the states required. Third, it is true that during severe recessions, the federal government has frequently enacted supplementary UI benefits that are entirely federally funded. But political support for using the Unemployment Insurance system during a recession is likely to be much greater than that for family assistance block grants because of the greater popularity of the clientele and availability of the Federal Unemployment Tax as a vehicle for raising offsetting revenues. But in one respect, experience with Unemployment Insurance is likely to be repeated with a family assistance block grant: the prospect of having to repay loans to the federal government with interest would probably spur states to cut eligibility and benefits to poor families at the height of a recession, just when their opportunities for labor market earnings would be weakest.[15] In short, a family assistance block grant is likely to transfer the risk of recession not just to states but on to poor families themselves.

If Congress decides to support a block grant system for supporting poor families, it is important to vary the amount of the grant with economic conditions in a state, perhaps using triggers similar to those in the current Unemployment Insurance Extended Benefits program. Because economic downturns also strain state budgets, there will be a strong temptation for states to use any additional federal funds to substitute for state funds. Thus any additional recession-triggered block grant should be contingent upon maintenance of state effort, and a modest state match of those additional federal funds.

Where Do We Go from Here?

In 1995, welfare reform politics has mostly been driven by the politics of spending reduction. The fixed-sum grant presented in both the House and Senate bills decreases in real value over time and protects the federal government from cost increases due to recessions, but it leaves the states holding the bag. Equally important, the block grant provisions are likely to encourage states to race to the bottom while failing to distribute funds equitably to them or produce balanced and carefully evaluated state welfare program innovations. The block grants will force states to shoulder an unfair share of the burden of economic downturns. In short, block grants are likely to make an admittedly bad situation far worse. Although the recommendations we have suggested as option A could mitigate these effects, the shortcomings of block grants remain sufficiently serious that we cannot recommend such a program.

These criticisms of block grants should not be cause to defend the status quo, however. There are reforms that could give the states more program leeway and the federal government more budgetary certainty. The use of waivers, which has already allowed states the freedom to experiment with AFDC and Medicaid dollars, should be expanded and encouraged. Welfare budgets could be established to keep total spending within acceptable bounds yet allow it to vary modestly with economic and demographic conditions. And finally, retaining the matching grant structure would preserve incentives for state contributions, but matching rates could be adjusted periodically to keep federal spending within limits. These changes will not produce massive, nearly painless savings, but neither will block grants.

3. A Primer on Welfare Reform

Rebecca M. Blank, Gary Burtless, William T. Dickens, LaDonna A. Pavetti, and Mark C. Rom

Research by social scientists has produced a lot of knowledge about both AFDC recipients and the effectiveness of programs intended to help recipients become self-sufficient. There is now a much better understanding, for example, of the duration of welfare spells and the effectiveness of a variety of welfare-to-work programs than was possible a few years ago. Much remains to be learned, however. In particular, very little is known about the likely effects of a number of reform proposals that have only recently been added to the policy agenda. This chapter reviews some of these findings — and gaps in current knowledge — in a question-and-answer format, and suggests some policy recommendations based on those findings.

The first sections of the chapter discuss problems associated with rising out-of-wedlock births and proposals to deal with these problems, as well as rising AFDC caseloads. Later sections of the chapter deal with the length of welfare spells and problems encountered in moving welfare recipients to self-sufficiency. The final sections of the chapter address inter-state competition and the potential for a "race to the bottom" in welfare eligibility and benefits.

What Are the Trends in Nonmarital Births?[*]

The share of births to unmarried mothers is rising as a share of all births. To understand why this is happening, it is important to distinguish between the *birthrate* among single and married women and the *number* of births to each group. The *nonmarital birthrate* shows the probability that a single woman will have a child. The *total number of nonmarital births* is the nonmarital birthrate multiplied by the number of single women in the population. Similarly, the total number of marital births is the marital birthrate multiplied by the number of married women. The "*illegitimacy ratio*," or the *share of nonmarital births*, is the total number of nonmarital births divided by all births (to both single women and married women). This ratio is affected by birthrates among both married and single women, as well as

---

[*]This section was written by Rebecca M. Blank.

by the number of single women relative to the number of married women in the population.

The birthrate of single women — the probability that a single woman will have a child — has actually declined among black women and remained relatively low among white women. The number of single women relative to the number of married women has grown enormously, however, at the same time as the birthrate of married women has declined. Each of these trends will be discussed in turn, and table 3-1 gives more detail on the numbers discussed here.

Fertility among married women has declined as family size has declined. In fact, the decline in family size among black married couples is even greater than that among white married couples. Declining fertility among married women is presumably not the problem most people are concerned with, although it has increased the share of out-of-wedlock births. If married couples are having fewer children, then even if there were no increase at all in the number of nonmarital births, the share of out-of-wedlock births would go up.

Among white women, the share of nonmarital births rose from 2 percent in 1960 to 21 percent in 1990 (see table 3-1). If white women's marital fertility had remained at its 1960 level, the share of nonmarital births for whites would have been only 13 percent, or 8 percentage points lower. Among black women, the share of nonmarital births rose from 23 percent in 1960 to 65 percent in 1990. If black women's marital fertility had remained at its 1960 level, the share of nonmarital births for blacks would have been 46 percent, or 19 percentage points lower.

Thus the raw data on the share of out-of-wedlock births overstate the problem. Declining marital fertility presumably represents a choice made by married couples that is not particularly worrisome. What does concern people is a rise in the *share* of nonmarital births caused by the rising *number* of nonmarital births, not the decline in the number of marital births.

The number of out-of-wedlock births has been rising, but the birthrate for single women has not changed much at all. Among all single white women, between 1960 and 1990 the probability of giving birth rose from 0.9 percent to 3.3 percent. Among all single black women, between 1960 and 1990 the probability of giving birth dropped from 9.8 percent to 9.0 percent. In other words, the probability that a single black women will have a child actually declined.

Table 3-1. Birth Rates and Number of Births to Single and Married Women, 1960-1990

	Single women			Married women			Overall (single & married) birth rate	Illegitimacy ratio: share of births to single women
	Birth rate per 1000	# Single women in (000s)	# Births to single women	Birth rate per 1000	# married women in (000s)	# births to married women		
All women 15-44								
1960	21.6	10,300	222,900	156.6	25,600	4,014,900	118.0	5.3%
1970	26.4	14,800	391,900	121.1	27,300	3,307,000	87.9	10.6%
1980	29.4	21,900	642,600	97.0	29,000	2,857,500	68.8	18.4%
1990	43.8	26,200	1,149,700	88.2	32,000	2,832,100	68.4	28.9%
White women 15-44								
1960	9.2	8,800	81,300	153.6	22,900	3,513,800	113.4	2.3%
1970	13.9	12,500	173,700	119.6	24,300	2,901,400	83.6	5.6%
1980	17.6	17,700	311,100	96.4	26,100	2,512,400	64.5	11.0%
1990	32.9	20,300	668,800	90.6	27,900	2,530,600	66.4	20.9%
Black women 15-44								
1960	98.3	1,500	146,200	180.9	2,800	499,600	150.2	22.6%
1970	95.5	2,200	205,500	130.3	2,700	355,100	114.4	36.7%
1980	82.9	3,700	307,900	94.4	2,700	256,100	88.1	54.6%
1990	90.5	5,000	448,600	82.8	2,900	239,500	87.1	65.2%
White teen women 15-19								
1960	6.6	4,930	32,538	513.0	772	396,036	75.2	7.6%
1990	30.6	6,475	198,135	398.1	377	150,084	50.8	56.9%
Black teen women 15-19								
1960	76.5	738	56,457	659.3	91	59,996	140.5	48.5%
1990	106.0	1,325	140,450	519.3	26	13,502	114.0	91.2%

Comparisons across columns may have small inconsistencies due to rounding.

1. Population data for 1990 are from U.S. Bureau of the Census, *Marital Status and Living Arrangements*, 1990; population data for 1960 are from U.S. Bureau of the Census, *Marital Status and Family Status*, 1960.

2. All birth rate data and the illegitimacy ratios were calculated by the author.

3. Natality data for 1960 are from U.S. National Center for Health Statistics, *Vital Statistics of the U.S., Volume I*, 1960; Natality data for 1990 is interpolated from the 1989 and 1991 data, where 1989 is from the U.S. National Center for Health Statistics, *Vital Statistics of the U.S., 1989, Volume I*, (Washington DC: GPO, 1993); and 1991 is from the U.S. National Center for Health Statistics, *Monthly Vital Statistics Report*, vol. 42, no. 3, (1993), pp. 29-30.

The main reason the number of births to single mothers is rising is that there are many more single women in the female population than before. Women are marrying later and divorcing sooner. Thus the rise in the number of nonmarital births is not occurring primarily because single women are more likely to have babies, but because there are simply more single women and hence more babies born to single women.

The trends among teenagers are somewhat different than the trends among all women (see table 3-1). *Overall* birthrates for teenagers are actually lower today than they were in 1960. Teenage birthrates dropped throughout most of the 1960s and early 1970s, but have been increasing since the mid-1980s.[16] The share of births to *unmarried* teenagers has soared, however, so that 60 percent of all births to white teenagers and 91 percent of all births to black teenagers are nonmarital births. This is because single teenagers are more likely to get pregnant than ever before *and* because fewer of them are marrying. In the past, many teenage women had children as married women. Almost all teenagers today who have children are not married and do not get married when they give birth.

This detailed discussion of the data is important because it changes the focus of the question. The main question is not "Why are teenagers (and other single women) having many more children than before?" Rather, the primary question should be "Why are teenagers (and other women) marrying much less than before?"

What Are the Causes Behind Declining Marriage Rates and Rising Numbers of Single Mothers?[*]

Conservative critics of the welfare system have argued that welfare payments are driving the increase in teenage pregnancy and the rising share of out-of-wedlock births. There is very little evidence supporting this claim, however. A wide variety of studies have assessed the relation between AFDC benefit payments and fertility. Depending on the study, the results indicate either that, once other variables are controlled for, AFDC payments are not related to women's fertility or that the effect is relatively small. Economist Robert A. Moffitt recently reviewed the research in this area. After extensively discussing all the studies, Moffitt concludes, "The failure to find strong benefit effects is the most notable characteristic of this literature."[17] Table 3-2 provides a summary of this literature.

Since racial differences are often invoked in the public discussion, it is worth noting that the research literature indicates that the relationship between benefit levels and fertility behavior is slightly stronger among low-income white women than

---

[*]This section was written by Rebecca M. Blank.

among African American women. Among black women, there is almost no persuasive evidence that benefit levels and nonmarital births are linked. There seems to be a weak positive link among white women.

Other evidence supports the conclusion that there is little relationship between welfare support levels and rising rates of out-of-wedlock births. *First, as many have noted, the monthly support levels available from AFDC and food stamps have fallen steadily since the late 1960s.* In 1970, the typical woman with three children and no other income would have received $900 a month (in 1992 dollars) from AFDC and food stamps combined — the primary public support programs that help pay the monthly bills. By 1990, the typical woman received around $700. It is hard to understand how the recent rapid increase in unwed motherhood can be fueled by public assistance payments when their levels have been declining. As noted in the section of this chapter on AFDC caseload increases, there has been a substantial increase in the real value of Medicaid benefits over time, but recipients generally value these benefits at less than their cost. Nor is it likely that gaining eligibility for Medicaid is a substantial factor in influencing the decisions of young women about whether to engage in sex, use birth control carefully, or bring to term and keep babies if they become pregnant.

Second, the rise in births among unwed mothers is not limited to those who rely on AFDC for support. It is a phenomenon spread throughout the income distribution. Although higher-income single women still have much lower rates of unwed births, their probability of giving birth has also risen substantially in the last twenty years. Nonmarital births have also risen in virtually every industrialized country in the world. Unwed motherhood is a social phenomenon that is related to many changing factors, from increased economic independence of women to decreased social stigma. To claim that it is primarily driven by welfare payments — available to only a small fraction of the U.S. population — is to miss the larger picture.

Third, the cross-national comparisons here are very revealing. Government support for single mothers is much lower in the United States than in other industrialized countries. Yet the United States has one of the higher rates of single motherhood and the highest rate of teenage pregnancy. For instance, Canada is similar to the United States in many ways, both economic and social. In the mid-1980s, Canada's public assistance programs for poor single mothers provided about twice as much support on average as those in the United States. Yet the illegitimacy rate in Canada continues to be below that in the United States.

Table 3-2. Recent Studies of the Effect of Welfare on Fertility

Study[18]	Data set	Analysis variable	Effect of welfare
Ellwood-Bane (1985)	1976 SIE	1. Had child in last year 2. Have children	None None
An-Haveman-Wolfe (1987)	1987 PSID	AFDC receipt for out-of-wedlock births	None
Winegarden (1988)	1947-83 DHHS and other government sources	Out-of-wedlock birth rate	Positive for nonwhites
Rank (1989)	1980-83 administrative data	1. Birth while on welfare 2. Fertility rate	Negative effect of length of time on welfare Women on welfare have lower fertility rate than total female population
Plotnick (1990)	1979-84 NLSY	1. Out-of-wedlock birth by age 19 2. Out-of-wedlock birth	Positive for whites None for nonwhites Positive for whites at first birth None for nonwhites
Duncan-Hoffman (1990)	1968-85 PSID	Out-of-wedlock birth associated with AFDC receipt	None
Lundberg-Plotnick (1990)	1979-86 NLSY	Premarital birth	Positive for whites None for blacks
Murray (1993)	1954-88 DHHS and other government sources	Illegitimacy ratio	Positive for whites Positive or negative for blacks depending on specification
Robins-Fronstin (1993)	1980-88 CPS	Number of children	Positive for whites and Hispanics Negative for blacks No effect of additional benefits for more children
Acs (1994)	1979-1988 NLSY	First and second births by age 23	Positive effect on first births for whites; no effect on second births

This is not to say that economic incentives are unimportant. On the margin, the evidence indicates that variations in birth levels have a weak relationship to variations in AFDC benefit levels, with stronger effects for white women than for black women. But, given the magnitude of the effects, there is no research evidence to support a conclusion that the presence of AFDC has been in any way the driving force behind large increases in births among unmarried women.

So what is the cause of rising out-of-wedlock births? Why has marriage among mothers declined? There are many overlapping factors, some of which affect specific subgroups of the population differently. Among these factors are the following:

1. Women's ability to find jobs and support themselves in the labor market has improved, increasing their economic independence. This has made marriage seem less attractive (it is no longer an economic necessity for many women) and single parenthood seems economically viable, especially for women with substantial education and marketable skills.

2. Men's ability to support a family, particularly among men with fewer formal skills, has declined. Among both high school dropouts and high school graduates, wage rates (adjusted for inflation) have declined substantially since the late 1970s, by 5 to 15 percent, depending on the skill level. This is due to a host of reasons, as the demand for less-skilled workers in our economy continues to decline.[19] The net effect is that men are less attractive as marriage partners.

3. The social stigma associated with unwed motherhood has declined. For many young women, particularly in the African American community, the acceptability of single parenthood has spread as more women have become single mothers. This has occurred at the same time as sexual activity outside of marriage has also become more common and widely acceptable in many parts of the population.

It is important to note that the growing economic independence of women and the decline in stigma associated with single parenthood has affected *all* women, and these two developments explain a rise in single parenthood among women of all income groups, consistent with the evidence. The decline in the labor market opportunities among less-skilled men primarily affects less-skilled women, due to marital sorting, and this explains higher levels of unwed motherhood among this group than among higher-income groups.

In summary, then, the primary causes of a decline in the propensity of women to marry are changes in the labor market and in the social acceptability of single parenthood, which has influenced women at all income levels. There is little evidence that the existence of cash assistance to low-income women has been anything but a minor factor behind the substantial increases in out-of-wedlock births. In fact, a long-term decline in the level of this assistance over the past twenty-five years — when the rise in out-of-wedlock births has been steepest — suggests that welfare is not a primary cause of rising single motherhood.

What Problems Are Associated with Single Parenthood, Especially among Teenage Mothers?[*]

Unmarried teenage mothers often face long-term economic struggle. This is particularly true if they drop out of school to raise their children, thereby limiting their future earnings opportunities. Rising rates of child poverty in the United States are primarily driven by the increase in the number of single mothers trying to raise children on their own.[20] While the majority of these women are divorced or separated, an increasing share have children outside of marriage.

The problems facing single-adult families are twofold. First, their economic opportunities are often limited. They have only one adult earner in the family, many single mothers have relatively low levels of education, and the jobs typically available to these women are low paying with limited opportunities for wage advancement. In addition, the presence of only one parent means that there is often no one to share the job of parenting, disciplining, and loving the children. The single parent who is trying to do it all often must face major economic and emotional burdens. These burdens are often multiplied when the single mother is also an adolescent, still coping with her own emotional, physical, and skill development.[21]

The problems of poor children in single parent families mirror those of their parents. Poverty, in and of itself, is bad for children. Regardless of family composition, poor children are more likely than non-poor children to be too short and too thin for their age. They develop academic skills more slowly than non-poor children, and are at higher risk of educational problems. There is also growing evidence that living with only one parent puts children at risk even when incomes don't differ. Children in single-parent families face greater problems of cognitive and physical development and are at higher risk of dropping out and becoming single parents themselves.[22]

Increases in the number of single-parent families have made it harder to bring people out of poverty through employment. It's easier for a two-adult family to escape poverty through work for a variety of reasons. Single-mother families have only one adult available for work, and that adult is also a single parent whose parenting responsibilities may constrain her work effort. Single-mother families often must pay child care when they go to work, requiring higher earnings to reach the same standard of living as a family where child care is provided costlessly by a second parent. Single mothers tend to be less skilled and are likely to be in jobs with low

---

[*]This section was written by Rebecca M. Blank.

wage levels. Finally, single mothers may also face more constraints on work hours because of concerns about safely getting to and from work late at night. With all of this, employment alone is likely to provide only limited support for single-mother families. Many working single-mother families need to have additional sources of income beyond their earnings in order to escape poverty.

Having emphasized many of the negative aspects associated with single motherhood, it is worthwhile to mention a few of the positive traits shown by poor single mothers. Unlike the absent fathers, these women stick with their children and typically work hard to raise them well. These women also work a substantial amount in the labor market, even if they don't earn enough to escape poverty. In fact, work hours among single mothers have risen slowly over time; single mothers work substantially more than married mothers.

While the economic problems facing single-parent families are substantial, a growing body of research provides increasing evidence that *teenage* mothers do not face substantially worse situations than other single mothers from similar backgrounds. Teenage mothers disproportionately come from lower-income homes and attend lower-quality schools. They are more likely to be African American or Hispanic. This suggests that their long-term earning power is likely to be limited, even if they did not have children at an early age. Recent studies have compared teenage mothers with their sisters, women who come from the same family and neighborhood but who did not have children before age twenty. The results indicate that by their mid-twenties, the earnings of teenage mothers are only slightly less than the earnings of their sisters who did not get pregnant as teenagers. By their mid-twenties, it's hard to tell who was an unwed teenage mother and who was not, not because the teenage mothers do particularly well, but because their sisters from the same family background do just as poorly.[23]

Other research supports these results, suggesting that teenage mothers work less and use more public assistance income in their early twenties, but they work *more* and use *less* public assistance in their late twenties than non-teenage mothers from similar backgrounds.[24] In other words, there is evidence that teenage parenting changes the timing of work and earnings for these women, but by their late twenties and early thirties, it is hard to say that teenage mothers are more disadvantaged than similar women who delayed childbearing. This suggests that the problems of unwed motherhood among young women may be less related to their childbearing, per se, than to the whole host of factors that limit their opportunities and make motherhood at age 15 or 16 more attractive than school or work.

Finding effective solutions to the problems that result from high rates of teenage pregnancy may require less focus on issues of sexual behavior and marriage, and more focus on issues of economic opportunity, adult role models, and a sense of possibility in the lives of young women *and* young men. Women with stronger educational aspirations, with a greater sense of future economic opportunities, and who perceive more choices in their lives are less likely to become teenaged mothers.

How Long do Families Stay on AFDC?[*]

Recent research on the length of time families stay on welfare indicates that it is extremely common for AFDC recipients to leave the rolls quickly. However, it is equally common for them to return almost as rapidly as they left.[25] Even taking account of multiple spells, the majority of families who ever receive AFDC benefits receive them for relatively short periods of time. On the other hand, a large fraction of those receiving AFDC *at any point in time* are likely to have been on for a long time and to continue receiving benefits for a long time. The difference between these two ways of looking at the relative importance of long spells results from the fact that the large number of families with short spells get on and off the rolls quickly while those with longer spells do not.

These points are illustrated in table 3-3. Column 1 presents the expected total time on welfare (over a lifetime) for families *first beginning* a spell of welfare receipt (new entrants). Column 2 presents the distribution of time mothers *currently receiving* AFDC can be expected to spend on the rolls over their lifetime, while column 3 presents the total time they have spent to date. These distributions provide answers to very different questions about the time families spend receiving welfare. However, the distinction between them is often misunderstood.

During fiscal year 1993, about 2.4 million applications for AFDC benefits were approved nationwide. The best estimates available indicate that close to half of these approved applications were for families who had never received assistance before (new entrants). The data presented in column 1 of table 3-3 provide an estimate of how much time these 1.2 million new recipients are expected to spend on the welfare rolls over their lifetime. For example, according to these estimates, 57.8 percent of these families will spend more than twenty-four months and 34.8 percent will spend more than sixty months on the welfare rolls. If one assumes that the distribution of time spent on the welfare rolls does not change from year to year, then this distribution can also be used to answer the question, "What percentage of recipients who *ever* turn to the welfare system for assistance will spend less than two years, more than five years, etc., on the welfare rolls?"

The distribution presented in column 2 is similar to column 1 in that it is also an estimate of *total time* spent on the welfare rolls. However, this distribution is for those recipients who are *currently* receiving benefits, not those who may have received

[*]This section was written by LaDonna A. Pavetti.

benefits in the past and have since left the rolls. This distribution is dramatically different from that for new entrants because long-term recipients are overrepresented on the caseload at a point in time. This occurs because the large number of short-term recipients who ever use welfare come and go while the long-term recipients are left behind.[26] Thus these data indicate that 90.7 percent of the 5 million families currently receiving AFDC benefits will eventually spend more than twenty-four months on the welfare rolls while 76.2 percent will eventually spend more than sixty months receiving welfare.

Rather than presenting estimates of the total time recipients spend on the welfare rolls, column 3 presents an estimate of the number of months recipients currently receiving welfare have spent on the welfare rolls *to date*. This distribution is often used to estimate the number of families who would be affected by policies to time-limit AFDC benefits. It indicates that if a twenty-four-month time limit were implemented today, 3.6 million families (71.1 percent) of the families receiving welfare would be cut off. Similarly, if a sixty-month time limit were implemented, 2.39 million families currently receiving benefits (47.8 percent of the current caseload) would be cut off.

The data presented in table 3-3 provide the best estimates currently available of the total time welfare recipients spend on the welfare rolls. However, it is important to note that these estimates are based on behavior of recipients under the current AFDC system. There is general agreement among social scientists that many of the proposed reforms would encourage some current AFDC recipients or would-be AFDC recipients to alter their behavior, thereby reducing the time some families will spend on the welfare rolls. However, because many of the proposed policy changes would radically alter the nature of the current AFDC program, there are no data currently available that can provide reliable estimates of how much less time recipients may spend on the welfare rolls under such policy changes.

Table 3-3. Time on Welfare for New Entrants and for the Caseload at a Point in Time

(Months unless otherwise indicated)

Time on welfare (in months)	New entrants (1)	Current Caseload Total expected duration of spells (2)	Total time on rolls to date (3)
1-12	27.4	4.5	16.4
13-24	14.8	4.8	11.9
25-36	10.0	4.9	9.5
37-48	7.7	5.0	7.8
49-60	5.5	4.5	6.6
60+	34.8	76.2	47.8
more than 24	57.8	90.7	71.7
Mean duration (years)	6.10	12.98	6.49

Source: These data are derived from a simulation model that uses monthly data to estimate movement on and off the welfare rolls over a twenty-five-year period. These estimates are similar to earlier estimates based on annual data. For a more detailed discussion of the model used to produce these estimates and a discussion of how these estimates compare with those derived using annual data, see LaDonna Pavetti, "Policies to Time-Limit AFDC Benefits: What Can We Learn from Welfare Dynamics?" Paper presented at the Institute for Social and Policy Studies, Yale University, November 30, 1994.

Who Spends Longer Periods of Time Receiving Welfare? Why Do People Who Leave Welfare for Jobs Return to the Welfare Rolls?[*]

Younger recipients, recipients who have never married, recipients who enter the welfare system with young children, and recipients with more than three children can all be expected to spend longer than average on the AFDC rolls (see table 3-4). African-American and Hispanic women are likely to have longer stays than their white counterparts. Most important, these data show a clear relationship between

---

[*]This section was written by LaDonna A. Pavetti.

preparation for the labor market and time on welfare: recipients with lower levels of education and no recent work experience can be expected to spend longer periods of time on welfare than more advantaged women.

Recipients who enter the welfare system before they have completed any high school (with less than nine years of schooling) have especially long stays on welfare: three-quarters of this group of recipients will spend more than two years and almost two-thirds will spend more than five years on the welfare rolls. Although this group makes up only a small fraction of those who ever turn to the welfare system for support, because their stays are so much longer than average they account for about 45 percent of recipients who will spend longer than two years and almost two-thirds of recipients who will spend longer than five years on the AFDC rolls.

Compare this with the experience of high school graduates. Fewer than one-half of them will spend more than two years on the welfare rolls, and only about one-quarter will spend more than five years. Women who have some high school fare worse than recipients who have completed high school but do substantially better than those with no high school: about two-thirds of this group will spend more than two years on the AFDC rolls and 40 percent will spend more than five years.

There is also a substantial difference in the welfare experiences of recipients who have worked recently and those who have not. Just over half of those recipients with recent work experience will spend more than two years on the welfare rolls, compared with two-thirds of those with no recent work experience. The difference in the percentage who will spend more than five years on the AFDC rolls is larger: 45 percent of recipients with no recent work experience compared with just over one-quarter of those with recent work experience. Recent work experience makes a substantial difference in the length of stay on the welfare rolls even for women with extremely low levels of education. More than 80 percent of recipients with low levels of education who did not work in the year before their initial welfare receipt spend more than two years on the welfare rolls, compared with just under two-thirds with recent work experience.

Even though these data clearly indicate that prior work experience and completion of high school increase the likelihood that a recipient will have a short stay on the welfare rolls, recent research on movement on and off the welfare rolls suggests that reducing the stays of longer-term recipients is likely to be much more complicated than simply finding jobs for low-skilled women with limited work experience.

Although early research concluded that relatively few single mothers left the welfare rolls because of an increase in earnings, recent work using better data has found that between one-half and two-thirds of all exits from welfare occur when a recipient gets paid work.[27] However, this research also finds that many of these exits into the labor market are extremely short-lived, with as many as 40 percent returning to AFDC within a year.[28]

Because it has long been assumed that few welfare recipients leave the rolls to enter the labor market, there is limited information available on the reasons why women who leave welfare for work return to welfare. The information that does exist is mostly anecdotal. It suggests that women return to the welfare system for a wide array of reasons that fall into three broad categories: job-related problems, work-family conflicts, and interpersonal problems.

Job-related problems include low pay, poor working conditions, no room for advancement, inadequate skills, and layoffs or other involuntary terminations. When women who participated in GAIN, California's employment and training program for welfare recipients, were asked why they left their jobs, 25 percent reported they were laid off and 21 percent reported that the job ended. Another 13 percent reported that they were fired, and the remaining 41 percent reported they quit.[29]

According to the evidence that is available, conflicts between work and family take a number of different forms: problems with child care (including reliability, quality and cost), medical problems (for both the former recipient and her children), housing instability, behavior and education problems of children, and domestic violence. While there is substantial evidence that personal and family problems play an important role in why women leave jobs to return to the welfare system, little has been done to date to determine the relative importance of these problems.

A study of job leaving among participants in Project Match, a welfare-to-work program serving residents of Chicago's Cabrini-Green Housing Project, provides the best evidence of how interpersonal problems play an important role in job loss among former welfare recipients. Interviews with program participants and employers revealed that disagreements or misunderstandings between coworkers or between workers and their supervisors often led to the termination of employment. The researchers concluded that problems that arose on the job often resulted from dramatic differences between the rules of the workplace and norms of behavior in the neighborhood where the program participants resided.[30]

The data presented in table 3-4, combined with the available information on why former recipients return to the welfare system, suggest that it may be quite difficult to move large numbers of welfare recipients *permanently* into the paid labor force. It is possible that if stricter work requirements were imposed, some recipients would leave welfare for work sooner than they might in the absence of such requirements. Similarly, recipients who leave welfare for employment might stay employed longer than they would under the current AFDC system. However, because the information is not currently available to determine how much job loss results because of the structure of the low-wage labor market and how much occurs because of personal circumstances beyond the control of the individual, it is impossible to predict how recipients who currently spend long periods of time on welfare will fare under a more stringent work requirement, especially if accompanied by a time limit on benefits.

Table 3-4. Time on Welfare For A Beginning Cohort of Recipients, by Selected Characteristics

Characteristics at beginning of first AFDC spell	All first-time recipients	Longer than 24 months on AFDC	Longer than 60 months on AFDC
All recipients	100.0	57.8	34.8
Education			
less than 9 years	13.0	75.3	63.4
9-11 years	34.0	66.2	40.0
12+ years	53.0	48.2	24.3
Work experience			
No recent	38.7	67.1	44.9
Recent	61.3	52.0	28.3
Age			
Under 24	52.7	64.5	41.9
25-30	24.9	51.9	25.6
31-40	19.3	48.4	28.3
Over 40	3.1	51.1	25.2
Race			
White/other	55.6	50.9	26.7
Black	28.4	66.4	41.4
Hispanic	16.0	66.9	50.7
Marital status			
Never married	58.2	65.5	43.1
Ever married	41.8	47.2	23.0
Age of youngest child			
less than 12 months	52.1	64.8	39.2
13-36 months	16.6	55.5	37.9
37-60 months	10.9	54.3	29.5
61-120 months	11.2	49.7	29.9
121+ months	9.3	37.1	15.2
Number of children			
1	57.2	57.0	35.8
2	33.2	58.2	31.9
3	7.5	58.7	35.9
3+	2.2	71.0	43.1

Source: These data are derived from a simulation model that uses monthly data to estimate movement on and off the welfare rolls over a twenty-five-year period. For a more detailed discussion of the model used to produce these estimates, see Pavetti, "Policies to Time-Limit AFDC Benefits."

Why Has the AFDC Caseload Increased?*

The history of AFDC caseloads from 1960 to 1994 are shown in figure 3-1. After increasing fairly steadily during the early and mid-1960s, the percentage of the U.S. population receiving AFDC increased abruptly between 1968 and 1972. Between 1972 and 1989, however, the number of AFDC recipients remained nearly unchanged, despite an 18 percent increase in the U.S. population.[31] In 1990 another brief period of rapid increase began. Between 1989 and 1993 the number of AFDC recipients increased by over 30 percent. By 1994 this growth seemed to have slowed or stopped. What accounts for the rapid growth in the 1960s, the fall in the 1970s and 1980s, and the abrupt increase in the early 1990s?

1960-72

Observers commonly attribute most of the increase in caseloads over the period from 1960 to 1972 to changes in program administration. A series of court decisions forced states to systematize the criteria for granting welfare benefits, removed caseworker discretion, and eliminated some restrictive rules.[32] The increases in these years are notable because incomes for all U.S. families — particularly the poor — were rising.

The value of welfare benefits also rose considerably during this period, mainly because of the large increases in the Food Stamp program and the phasing in of Medicaid. But most of the increases in benefits came late in the period after most of the caseload increase had already taken place.

Changes in family structure played little role in the increases in welfare caseloads during the early to late 1960s. From 1960 to 1968 the fraction of the population receiving AFDC benefits increased by over 75 percent while the ratio of the number of female-headed households to the population as a whole increased by only 6 percent. Even in the later years of this period, when changing family structure played a larger role in the increasing caseload, it was still a less important factor than the increasing use of AFDC by female-headed families. From 1968 to 1972 the fraction of the population receiving AFDC benefits increased by over 50 percent while the ratio of female-headed families to the population increased by only 16 percent.

---

*This section was written by William T. Dickens.

Figure 3-1. AFDC Recipients and Unemployment, 1960-94

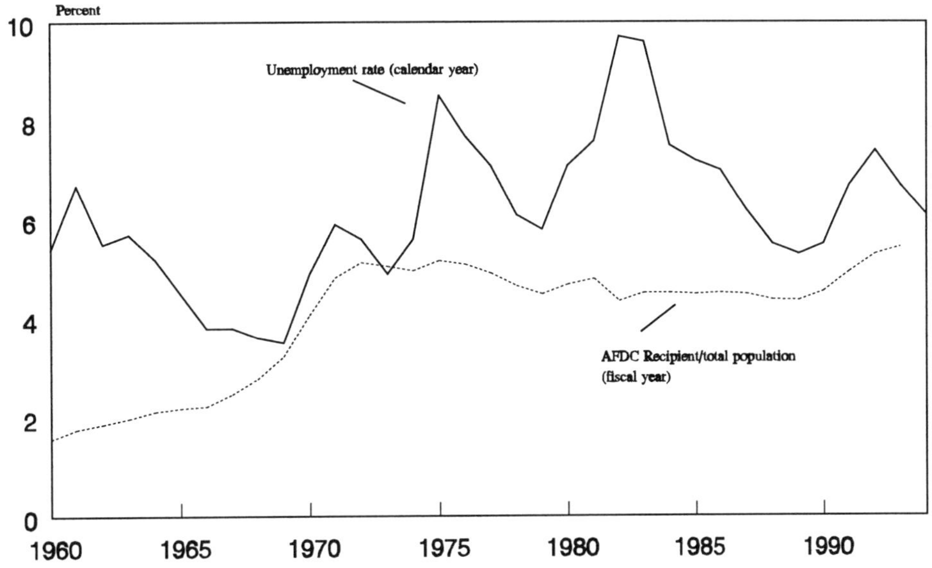

Sources: *Employment and Earnings*; and *Green Book*, various years.

1972-89

The period of 1972 to 1989 was one of relative stability in AFDC caseloads. While the number of cases varied from year to year, the fraction of the population receiving benefits fell by 17 percent over the period. This decline took place despite an increase of over 70 percent in the ratio of female-headed families to the population and a near tripling of the ratio of families headed by never-married mothers to the population as a whole. Never-married mothers are much more likely to get on and stay on welfare than divorced mothers.

A large part of the decline in caseloads is often attributed to the fall in the real value of AFDC benefits over the period. The money value of benefits was infrequently increased in the face of considerable inflation. For example, the average benefit received by a family of four declined from about $798 a month in 1972 to about $568 a month in 1989 after adjusting for inflation.[33]

However, the value of Medicaid services increased greatly over this same period, and Food Stamp payments increased, partially offsetting the decline in AFDC benefits. As a result, the sum of AFDC payments, Food Stamps and the average value of medicaid services used by AFDC recipients increased from $1,087 a month for a family of four in 1972 to $1,197 a month in 1989 after adjusting for inflation.[34] Those who argue that the decline in benefits explains the fall in use argue that Medicaid benefits are valued at substantially less than their cost by the poor. The inflation-adjusted value of cash plus Food Stamp benefits alone fell by nearly 20 percent over these years.

Another part of the explanation for the decline in the fraction of people using AFDC over this period is changes in eligibility requirements — in particular the tightening that occurred in the early years of the Reagan administration, when many people who were working and receiving AFDC were made ineligible for the program. The number of AFDC recipients fell by nearly a million from 1981 to 1982 despite the severe 1982 recession. Together with the decline in the value of cash benefits, these changes can account for nearly all of the decline in utilization.

1989-1994

While there are satisfying explanations for the changes through 1989, the rapid increase in the use of AFDC after 1989 remains a mystery. Most of the explanations that have been advanced can be easily dismissed, while the ones that remain are speculative at best.

Several observers have suggested that the recent rapid increase in the number of families headed by never-married mothers explains the increase in caseloads.[35] However, between 1989 and 1994 the number of families headed by never-married mothers increased by 577,000 while the AFDC basic caseload increased by over 1 million families.[36] Since less than half of all families headed by never-married mothers receive AFDC at any time, the increase can account for only a small fraction of the total caseload increase. Further, although the number of families headed by never-married mothers increased rapidly during this period, the number has been increasing rapidly for the last two decades.[37] This long term trend alone cannot explain the rapid increase in the years in question.

Nor can the 1990 recession explain the increase. As can be seen from figure 3-1, increases in the unemployment rate are normally associated with very slight increases in the AFDC caseload. The increase in unemployment during the 1974-75 recession was much larger and sharper than that of the 1990-91 recession, but the increase in caseloads was less dramatic. Further, by early 1995 unemployment rates had returned to their prerecession levels, but caseloads remained high. If the 1990 recession explains the increase it must be because the recession was very different from past recessions or because some change in the AFDC system has made caseloads *much* more sensitive than in the past.

Although the value of AFDC and Food Stamps combined continued to decline over this period (from $742 a month in 1989 to $702 in 1994), the value of Medicaid increased considerably. Over these years poor families used more medical services and the price of medical services rose faster than the prices of other goods, so the inflation adjusted value of Medicaid services consumed by a typical AFDC household rose from $454 a month in 1989 to $632 a month in 1992 (the most recent year for which data are available). Thus the total dollar value of AFDC, Food Stamps, and Medicaid rose by over 14 percent while the fraction of the population receiving AFDC rose by 22 percent. Even if AFDC recipients valued Medicaid services at their cost, this increase could explain only about a quarter of the total increase (given standard estimates of the response of caseloads to benefits), and it is usually assumed that Medicaid benefits are valued at only a third to a half of their dollar cost.

Administrative changes are thought to have had profound impacts on caseloads in the past, so the changes made as a result of the Family Support Act of 1988 are prime suspects for explaining the subsequent caseload growth. The major provisions of the act set up the Job Opportunities and Basic Skills training program (JOBS) and put in place a requirement that AFDC recipients must be working, seeking work, or taking part in a training program.

One might expect that putting additional requirements on welfare recipients would reduce caseloads, as should job training, if successful. However, sanctions for failure to take part in the JOBS program are seldom enforced. And, although job training provided under the program passes a cost-benefit test, it does very little to reduce caseloads. Further, the offer of job training (and child care) to AFDC recipients may have attracted some people onto AFDC. But it seems unlikely that this could explain much of the growth in caseloads since the average value of JOBS benefits per AFDC family is considerably less than $37 a month.[38]

Further, states have differed considerably in how quickly and completely they have implemented JOBS, and the correlation between the fraction of the caseload participating in JOBS and the rate of growth of caseloads over this period is slightly negative, suggesting that the Family Support Act may have reduced the rate of growth of caseloads somewhat.

Another possible, but unlikely, explanation of AFDC caseload growth is increased dependency on crack cocaine. This drug is thought to have had a particularly devastating effect on poor neighborhoods. Use of this cheap and potent form of an old drug grew to epidemic proportions in the mid- to late-1980s. This explanation is unlikely because of the timing of the two events. "Crack first appeared in American cities in 1985 and peaked in 1988," according to the U.S. Department of Justice.[39] Both the use of cocaine and drug-related crime rose sharply during the mid-1980s but began falling sharply in 1989.[40] The increase in caseloads began a year after the crack problem began to abate.

A final possible explanation for the caseload boom is that efforts in several states to promote the use of Medicaid by the working poor may have led some people to apply for AFDC. It is true that states that had large growth in AFDC caseloads also had large growth in Medicaid caseloads, but this would have been expected in any case since any family eligible for AFDC is eligible for Medicaid. The explanation is questionable since the purpose of the outreach was to acquaint people with new rules that made it possible for them to continue Medicaid coverage for a year while employed after a spell on AFDC. However, final judgment on this explanation awaits a full analysis of how the intensity of promotional activities correlates with caseload growth.

Conclusion

Growth in AFDC caseloads over the last three and a half decades is surprisingly uneven. While the pattern of changes from 1960 to 1989 is understandable, there is no more than a partial explanation for the recent dramatic increase in caseloads. The history of caseload changes has several lessons for welfare reform.

1. Changes in how the program is administered can have large effects on caseloads. It will be very difficult to project the effects of radical reforms on program cost.

2. Changes in the value of benefits have notable effects on caseloads, although they cannot explain more than a small fraction of any of the sharp increases in caseloads that have occurred. Because the effects of benefit changes on family structure and fertility appear to be low and uncertain, this effect probably occurs largely through choices of work versus welfare.[41] To the extent that welfare reform leads to lower benefits per family, there will be a moderate and predictable decline in program costs.

3. More children born out of wedlock need not mean larger welfare rolls. The numbers of families headed by never-married mothers increased steadily from the mid-1960s on, but for long stretches of time caseloads shrank or remained constant. Other factors, such as the level of benefits and the details of eligibility, are as important as the underlying demographic trends in explaining caseload growth. Care should be taken when drawing conclusions about the implications of demographic changes for program cost.

4. Both the long- and short-term changes in the economic circumstances of the poor affect caseloads, but their effects are remarkably small. Major improvements in economic well-being during the 1960s coincided with large increases in caseloads, while the marked deterioration of opportunities for those at the bottom end of the income distribution in the 1980s coincided with a fall in the fraction of the population using AFDC. Further, there are no good explanations for the most recent 30 percent

increase in welfare caseloads. The fact that such a change can happen so rapidly with no apparent precipitating cause should caution those who wish to put the entire burden of uncertainty about future caseloads on states.

What Will Be the Effect of Limiting or Abolishing Public Assistance for Children Born to Unmarried Teenage Mothers?*

H.R. 4, the welfare reform bill passed by the House of Representatives in March, would bar the use of federal block grant funds to pay cash public assistance for teenage mothers who bear children outside of marriage, although it would permit the issuance of vouchers to teenage mothers to be used for the purchase of diapers, cribs, and other commodities. The House-passed bill would also allow states to use their own funds to pay cash benefits to teen mothers, and the governor of at least one major state, New Jersey, has indicated that her state would continue cash payments.[42] The bill introduced by Senate Majority Leader Robert Dole would permit states to deny family assistance payments to teen mothers (also until they reach age 18), but would not require them to do so.

Any sort of teen mother exclusion will make it much more difficult for single mothers to survive economically; the extent of that increased deprivation clearly depends on the exact nature of the provisions enacted and, where there are state options to use federal funds or their own funds, the decisions made by the states. All of the following effects are likely to occur in the event of enactment of a teen mother exclusion:

1. *Fewer women will have children as single mothers, either because they engage in less extramarital sex, because they use birth control more consistently, or because they are more likely to have abortions if they become pregnant.* Given evidence currently available, it is impossible to say exactly how big this effect would be. Based on what is known about current teenage sexual behavior and the small weight that young men and women often give to future consequences, it is likely that substantial numbers of out-of-wedlock births will continue to occur.

2. *Women who continue to give birth to children will be less likely to live independently.* More of them will live with other family members (such as parents or sisters), will live with boyfriends, or will choose to marry. Again, it is hard to predict the size of this effect.

It is important to note that these choices may not do anything to solve poverty among these women and their children. Many poor women, in particular, have

---

*This section was written by Rebecca M. Blank.

families and boyfriends who are also quite poor. Many poor women and their children are likely to end up in more crowded housing situations, where more people live together and pool income but the larger total household is still quite poor. In addition, it is important to note that the incidence of domestic abuse among low-income women seems to be quite high. The state of Washington, in a study of a random sample of all its AFDC recipients, found that fully 60 percent reported a history of sexual or physical abuse as adults, from either family members or boyfriends.[43] This is far above the incidence of physical and sexual abuse in the general population. Thus moving women back into more shared housing arrangements may increase such problems for both the women and their children.

3. A number of women will try to maintain their independence and survive economically without public assistance. Most of these women will work more hours. Some of this will be in mainstream legitimate employment, and some of it will be in illegal employment. The evidence available about the low-wage labor market facing the least-skilled women is that many of them are unable to find jobs that fully replace public assistance. This is particularly true since many women need to pay child care expenses if they have preschoolers at home or if they work while their children are home from school. Some of these women, particularly those with no family available to help, will find themselves out of work, or in jobs that simply can not pay the rent. These women, in the absence of public support, will turn up among the homeless.

Evaluations of the effects of increased hours of work among women in states running welfare-to-work programs indicate that these programs increase women's hours of work and decrease their reliance on AFDC, but that their overall change in income is quite small. In other words, few less-skilled women can earn enough in the labor market to do more than just replace public assistance income unless they greatly increase their hours of work.

More labor market work has obvious implications for single parents who must also serve as sole parent for their children. Adult presence, discipline, and oversight in the household will decline. In less-safe neighborhoods, where children are at risk of street violence and gang participation, this may result in very bad outcomes for some children and their families.

What is the net effect of cutting welfare payments for young unmarried women? Those who claim it will decrease motherhood among single women and will increase marriage rates are surely right. Those who claim that a substantial number of never-married women will still choose to have children and that these women and their children will almost surely be poorer are also right. The question is how big these effects will be. Since no state has ever implemented a teen mother exclusion, there is no direct evidence on the relative magnitude of these effects.

The Department of Health and Human Services has estimated that when the House-passed ban on benefits to teenage mothers and their children while the mother is still under age 18 is fully implemented, 80,000 children will lose their benefits.[44] If it resulted in a substantial decline in births, the number would be smaller. Even if nonmarital births were to decline by 50 percent after restrictions on welfare payments to unmarried mothers are implemented — an enormously and unbelievably large effect — a very large number of unmarried women and their children will be affected. Most of them will be poorer and more desperate than they were before.

The potential costs to poor children of a teen mother exclusion and the absence of evidence about how much it would affect births to teen mothers suggest that a national mandate of such a policy would be irresponsible. Efforts to test teen mother exclusion policies on a small scale encounter distinctive problems, however. Traditional research methods of random assignment to control and treatment groups within the same community are likely to provide misleading results, since the full potential of a teen mother exclusion is likely to be achieved only if teenagers receive very powerful, consistent messages that they will not receive family assistance payments if they become pregnant. These considerations suggest that a statewide test is probably the minimum practical test.

Statewide tests, or allowing teenage mother exclusions as a state option, also pose serious problems, however. The most important is a heightened potential for migration from states where teenagers are not eligible for benefits to those where they are. Indeed, New Jersey officials have publicly voiced fears that any attempt by their state to avoid a teen mother exclusion would be unsustainable if neighboring states did not follow suit, because New Jersey would become a magnet for desperate families from those states.[45] The same sorts of "race to the bottom" effects would likely arise if states were permitted the option of having a higher exclusion age limit than age 18, as permitted in earlier versions of the House bill.

Overall, these considerations suggest that *if* teenage mother exclusion policies are to be tested, the test should be on a limited statewide basis, under federally granted waivers, with a careful evaluation of the consequences.

What Effects do Family Caps Have?[*]

Many believe that women who conceive children while receiving AFDC are taking advantage of the system. Consequently, rules that deny additional benefits in such cases (often called "family caps") are quite popular (see chapter 6 on public opinion toward family caps). Advocates of these provisions say that they are trying to

---

[*]This section was written by William T. Dickens.

send a strong message that conceiving an additional child while on welfare is not acceptable behavior. They also argue that such provisions may reduce additional births to AFDC mothers, and ultimately shrink caseloads and thus the fiscal burden of AFDC programs. Opponents of caps have argued that the cuts are overly harsh and affect innocent children as well as their mothers. Others are concerned that caps may increase the number of abortions among women on AFDC. What will be the effects of family caps?

There are three places to look for evidence on the likely effects of family caps on fertility; together, they suggest that caps may have modest effects or no effects at all. The most obvious and important source is the recent experience of New Jersey, the first state to institute such a cap, and the only state where a cap has been in effect long enough to provide meaningful evidence.

In August 1993 New Jersey prohibited women from receiving increases in their AFDC payments for children born more than ten months after they begin receiving AFDC. At the same time the state also introduced a number of other changes to its welfare program, including some to improve job prospects for AFDC recipients.

Effects on Incomes

Before the introduction of the New Jersey family cap, the monthly benefit of a recipient with one child who had a child while on AFDC would have increased from $308 to $401. With the family cap in effect, benefits do not increase, so benefits would be 23 percent less than they would have been before the cap.

This seems very large, but almost no one receives only AFDC, and some other benefits will increase as AFDC decreases (most notably food stamps). June O'Neill computed the average cash and noncash income of AFDC recipients from a wide range of government programs and concluded that the income of a woman who had a second child while on AFDC would be about 5 percent lower as a result of the cap.[46] Families with more than one child before the additional birth would see a considerably smaller percentage loss in total income. Different assumptions about which programs a family participates in make only a few percentage points of difference in this conclusion.

Effects on birth rates

It is possible to compare the birthrates of women on AFDC before and after the introduction of the family cap and the other changes as a test of their effects. In addition, the state of New Jersey was required by the Department of Health and Human Services (HHS) to set up a random assignment test of the cap in which some individuals were exempted from the provisions of the cap in order to create a comparison or "control group" whose experience could be compared with those who were subject to the cap.

At this point the evidence on the New Jersey experience is mixed. Preliminary results from the random assignment experiment suggested that births among those subject to the cap had decreased by as much as 20 percent.[47] However, a more recent study of the experimental groups, using more complete data on births, has reportedly found no statistically significant difference between the birthrates of those subject to the cap and those not subject to it.[48] Those conducting the later study think that better birth data are the main reason for the difference between their findings and those of the earlier study, but they have not yet released their study, and there are other differences in the analysis between the two studies that also might account for some of the difference in results. More information should be available later in 1995.

Whatever the results of the experiment, there is no question that something caused the fertility of New Jersey's AFDC population to drop abruptly at the time of the adoption of the family caps. Although the drop in fertility has not been as pronounced in more recent months (14 percent during the first six months of the program, compared with about 9 percent for the six months ending in October 1994),[49] it is still apparent.

How does one reconcile these seemingly contradictory findings? First, the adoption of the cap was not the only aspect of the New Jersey welfare system that was changed. It is possible that the drop in fertility results from other aspects of the New Jersey reforms or perhaps some synergy between different reforms. The experiment tests only the effects of the cap.

Alternatively, the before-and-after comparison may provide a more accurate measure of the effect of the law than the experimental comparisons. The control group in the experiment is living in a state in which the community has made clear its feelings about women on AFDC having more children. Further, the experimental groups are sufficiently small that the experiment could not reliably detect a change in fertility of the magnitude suggested by the before-and-after data.[50]

Before-and-after data also suggest an increase in the abortion rate.[51] About a quarter of the drop in births among welfare recipients seems to have been due to an increase in the abortion rate.

Two other types of studies also suggest that caps might slightly reduce the birthrate of women receiving AFDC, though again the evidence is mixed. Studies of the effects of welfare benefits on fertility among unmarried women and studies of pronatalist policies in other countries both provide additional evidence that should be considered. Although results are not consistent across studies, and no formal assessment of the joint significance of the results from all studies has been done, many studies show positive effects of economic incentives on fertility.[52]

Effects on State Budgets

The effects of the cap on AFDC caseloads and expenses are difficult to compute, but evidence suggests that it is small at best. Estimating the effect would require modeling the flow in and out of the AFDC system as well as the effects of the cap on family composition. However, the cap seems to be causing a drop of at most 3,000 births a year in a state with a welfare population of more than 300,000 recipients. It seems unlikely that the cap will reduce welfare costs by more than a few percentage points.

The long term consequences of family caps are uncertain. It is possible that the effects of the cap will grow over time if the rule affects community norms. On the other hand, the effects may decline as publicity about the changes fades.

Taken together, existing evidence suggests that family caps have only modest effects on fertility and family well being. Support for family caps should not be based on an expectation that they will save money. On the other hand, family caps do communicate the community's sense that conceiving additional children while receiving public assistance is an unfair abuse of the social safety net, and they do so without imposing overwhelming costs on recipients.

What Is the Proper Balance among Various Types of Welfare-to-Work Programs?*

Skill deficiencies are an important reason why welfare recipients cannot find good jobs. Programs that provide education, job training, or earnings subsidies can offer a partial solution to this problem. A variety of work and training programs for welfare recipients have been attempted over the past few decades. Analysts have accumulated a large amount of evidence about programs that succeed in improving recipients' earnings and the reasons for program success and failure. Much of this evidence suggests that education, training, and job placement programs can be worthwhile for some groups of recipients. None of it suggests that these programs, by themselves, can lift many long-term recipients out of poverty.

How the Programs Work. Most people (and most policymakers) think the main goal of welfare-to-work programs should be to prepare unskilled workers for the labor

---

*This section was written by Gary Burtless.

market. Welfare recipients are taught how to search for jobs, are required to file job applications with a variety of employers, are enrolled in basic education and training programs, or have their wages subsidized in private-sector jobs. If a program succeeds, it is reasonable to assume welfare recipients will find jobs and leave the welfare rolls. If the program fails, recipients will remain jobless and dependent on welfare.

The programs may affect entry to or exit from the welfare rolls in another way, however. If the work and training program is believed by participants to be time-consuming or burdensome, some potentially eligible adults will be deterred from applying for AFDC. Others who are already receiving public assistance may exit the rolls sooner than they otherwise would even if they do not find a job. When recipients are required to participate in an ineffective or burdensome program as a condition for obtaining cash aid, a small percentage of potential applicants may decline to enroll in AFDC or may leave welfare sooner than they would if participation in the program were voluntary.

Of course, some kinds of welfare-to-work programs offer AFDC recipients valuable benefits, such as child care subsidies and extended Medicaid eligibility. Some low-income parents may find these ancillary benefits attractive and apply for AFDC benefits in order to gain access to them. Other AFDC participants may remain on the welfare rolls longer than they otherwise would in order to take full advantage of any special training that is offered. Current proposals to reform welfare are unlikely to achieve these kinds of effects. Most reforms are intended to impose extra obligations on welfare recipients and hence will make AFDC benefits less attractive.

Employment-oriented programs can thus achieve notable results through two routes: by improving the job qualifications of program participants or by discouraging potential AFDC recipients from entering or remaining on the rolls. Either kind of effect can reduce the cost of public assistance payments, but only the first one is likely to produce an improvement in the standard of living of low-income families. The second effect can yield significant taxpayer savings, but it is likely to reduce the net incomes of families collecting public aid. The success of alternative welfare-to-work strategies must be judged by which goal is considered most important: improving participants' living standards or reducing taxpayer burdens.

Job placement. The most common (and least expensive) work-oriented strategy is to enroll recipients in a job search program. Search programs may combine mandatory instruction in job-finding techniques with a formal, intensive, and systematic program of job seeking. These programs typically require that participants spend several hours a day or week engaged in search-related activities (preparation of résumés, telephoning prospective employers, and pounding the pavement to find job leads). By assumption, the job seeker is already capable of performing some jobs, though the jobs may be menial and poorly paid.

The virtue of job search programs from an administrative perspective is that the obligation to look for work can be enforced easily and inexpensively. A minimal program might require that AFDC recipients bring signed statements from half a dozen employers each week confirming the recipient has filed formal job applications.

A number of demonstrations and classical experiments in the 1980s showed that mandatory job search programs can be a cost-effective way to raise employment rates and reduce the welfare rolls. The effects of the programs, however, are usually modest. The most successful program to rely mainly on immediate job placement through job search assistance is California's GAIN program, as implemented in Riverside County. In its first three years, the program increased employment rates among targeted AFDC recipients by 14 percentage points (or about 25 percent of the control group average) and boosted average earnings by slightly more than $1,000 a year. AFDC payments to targeted recipients fell 15 percent, or roughly $660 a year. (These estimates reflect program effects on single parents collecting AFDC. The effects on two-parent households were somewhat smaller.) The Riverside job search program was unusually well managed and successful. Other job search programs have achieved more modest effects, often less than half those registered in Riverside County. Nonetheless, many of the less expensive programs are judged cost-effective from the point of view of taxpayers, because less government money is spent on administering the job search requirement than is saved in AFDC and food stamp costs. AFDC recipients should be less happy with the outcome, because their net earnings gains often fall short of their loss of AFDC and food stamp benefits. Well-run programs succeed in reducing AFDC costs and caseloads, but they usually fail to improve the living standards of participants.[53]

Basic education. The educational attainment of AFDC recipients, though improving, is far below average. A 1991 government survey found that fewer than 55 percent of AFDC mothers had completed high school. In comparison, more than 85 percent of all American women aged 25-34 had completed high school. About 1 percent of AFDC mothers have graduated from college, whereas 23 percent of all women aged 25-34 have a college degree. The educational shortcomings of AFDC recipients are also reflected in very poor performance on standardized tests of ability and achievement. Among 25-year-old women collecting AFDC year-round, more than 70 percent score in the bottom quarter of all test takers.[54]

One possible remedy for these educational deficiencies is adult basic education, especially education leading to a high school equivalency degree. During the early implementation of the GAIN program, this was a favored strategy in several California counties. There is little evidence to suggest the approach was particularly successful, however. California counties that emphasized enrollment in adult basic education programs did not achieve better results than other counties. They almost certainly achieved worse results than Riverside County, which emphasized immediate placement in jobs through job search and short-duration employment training.[55]

However, it is conceivable that the longer-term benefits of adult basic education may not be visible in a demonstration program that lasts only two or three years. Participants in adult education may sacrifice immediate earnings while they are enrolled in the schooling program for longer-term gains that do not become noticeable until a few years after the schooling ends.

Research on the effects of adult education suggests this is unlikely, though. Recent studies by University of Chicago economist James Heckman imply that attainment of a high school equivalency degree by a high school dropout has a very small labor market payoff. Adults who have received a tenth grade education and a GED earn only slightly more than adults with the same level of schooling who have not received the GED diploma.[56] One reason that adult basic education yields such meager earnings improvements might be that enrollment in a schooling program diverts adults from an activity that offers positive labor market benefits — actual job experience.

Occupational Training. Another strategy to improve AFDC recipients' employability is to enroll them in short-term occupational training. This approach has been emphasized in a number of demonstration programs and continues to be important in the Job Training Partnership Act (JTPA). The strategy can be more costly than adult basic education and is nearly always more expensive than job search assistance programs. Careful research studies, including classical experiments, often show that this approach to job preparation for female AFDC recipients can be successful, but the employment and earnings gains enjoyed by participants are seldom large. Earnings gains only rarely average as much as $1,500 a year; gains half this large are more typical. The earnings gains from this strategy seem to be concentrated among a comparatively small percentage of participants. Many gain little from their training and do not end up in jobs that use the specialized training that was offered in the program.[57]

There is less evidence about the benefits of costly, long-term occupational training for welfare recipients. The most expensive programs, including Supported Work and the Homemaker-Home Health Aide training project, achieved larger average earnings gains than less costly programs, but these programs were made available to *volunteers* from the AFDC rolls. It is not obvious these costly programs would have achieved such impressive results if AFDC recipients had been required to participate in them as a condition for receiving AFDC. The success of these comparatively expensive occupational training programs suggests, however, that offering the option of a challenging and costly occupational training program to AFDC recipients can be beneficial for some of them.[58]

Community service jobs. Unpaid community service employment (or workfare) is one of the costliest work-oriented strategies.[59] It requires program administrators to find supervisors, safe job sites, and real work opportunities for welfare recipients. It also requires fairly elaborate administrative procedures to ensure that recipients show up for their jobs, work diligently during assigned hours, and receive penalties if they do not meet their work obligations. While a number of experimental programs have instituted community work experience programs, participation in these programs usually turns out to be rare. For example, in an Arkansas experiment only 3 percent of welfare recipients enrolled in the experimental treatment actually participated in a workfare job. The comparable percentage in an Illinois experiment was 7 percent; in a Virginia experiment, 10 percent; and in a San Diego experiment, 20 percent.[60]

It might seem odd that so many recipients are called to participate in these workfare programs, but so few actually chose (or were forced) to participate. Many people enrolled in the experiment probably had reasonable excuses for their nonparticipation. Others left the welfare rolls before a workfare position could be found. Still others participated in some alternative activity, like education, job training, or a part-time job, that precluded their participation in workfare. But many failed to show up on a workfare job without any good reason.

In a welfare program with strict time limits on cash assistance, community work experience can play a useful role. First, it might provide some parents with useful job experience that helps them later find unsubsidized jobs. Even more important, welfare recipients who exhaust their eligibility for cash aid without finding an unsubsidized job can be placed in a *paid* community job as a last-resort method of earning income. For some welfare recipients this may be the only feasible way to enforce a work obligation if indigent children are to be kept united with their single parents. In the absence of community work experience jobs or continuing cash aid, some single mothers with no work qualifications may simply be incapable of providing financial support for their children.

Earnings subsidies. Government officials have tried two variants of earnings subsidy programs to help welfare recipients find work. Under one plan, employers are offered subsidies if they give jobs to welfare recipients. Under the second, welfare recipients themselves collect the earnings subsidy.

The first form of subsidy has a very uneven record of success. One of the most successful programs run under JTPA is the on-the-job-training (OJT) subsidy program. Employers are granted a subsidy for training workers who are referred by the local JTPA agency. Although employers are not obligated to keep subsidized workers on their payrolls when the subsidy ends, many employers do. This approach to job training yields large and statistically significant gains in employment and earnings for workers who are lucky enough to be placed. Unfortunately, program administrators have difficulty finding many employers willing to offer positions. As a result, this strategy can be used in only a limited number of cases.[61]

The Targeted Jobs Tax Credit (TJTC) and welfare grant diversion represent alternative ways to subsidize employers for hiring welfare recipients. These programs do not oblige employers to provide training to subsidized workers. Employers are required only to offer jobs in order to collect the subsidy. Economists have found little evidence to suggest either program has led to improvements in welfare recipients' employment or earnings. Two classical experiments that tested the effectiveness of the TJTC found that employers were *less* likely to offer jobs to welfare recipients once they learned that the recipients were covered by the TJTC subsidy. Perversely, the offer of an earnings subsidy reduced the chances an employer would offer welfare recipients a job.[62]

The second type of earnings subsidy is one that is paid directly to welfare recipients who find jobs, rather than to their employers. The Earned Income Tax Credit (EITC) is the best known plan of this type. Although in theory the credit should increase the incentive for welfare recipients to find work, the actual effects of the credit on behavior are unknown. Even if the credit has no effect on participants' behavior, it can provide a major boost to their after-tax incomes. In 1994, the maximum credit for a family with two children amounted to slightly more than $2,500 a year, or about $50 a week. For a parent earning the minimum wage who works on a full-time schedule, this represents one-third of the net hourly wage available without the credit. In view of the sizable decline in real wages paid to unskilled workers, the increased generosity of the EITC is one of the few bright spots in an otherwise dismal economy.

Overview. The evidence from recent evaluation studies shows that good employment and training programs can significantly boost the earnings of welfare recipients and can do so in a cost-effective way. That is, they can raise participants' earnings by enough to offset the direct and indirect cost of administering the programs. But the evidence also offers a less encouraging lesson. Even the most successful programs fail to raise earnings enough to make a large difference in the poverty of poor mothers and their children. Some programs caused participants' earnings to rise by a third or more. Unfortunately, this large percentage gain does not translate into a substantial improvement in most recipients' standard of living. The reason is simple: people on welfare earn very little money. Even if their wages doubled or tripled, few would earn close to the amount needed to bring their families up to the poverty line. A number of programs have been found to work; none has been found to work miracles.

How Much Work Should Be Expected of AFDC Mothers? What Supportive Services Are Needed to Increase Their Labor Force Participation?*

All recent proposals to reform welfare aim to move AFDC recipients off the welfare rolls and into the work force. The great majority of families receiving AFDC are headed by single mothers, many of whom face formidable obstacles to holding full-time jobs. How realistic is the goal of moving a large percentage of dependent single mothers from welfare rolls into jobs? What kinds of single mothers would find the transition difficult? Which mothers would find the move into jobs easiest? What types of public support are needed to make the transition to work feasible?

Preparation for Work and Recent Job Experience

One way to assess the job prospects of welfare recipients is to examine the job qualifications and actual work experience of AFDC mothers. The U.S. Department of Health and Human Services periodically publishes information about the characteristics, including work behavior, of AFDC recipients using data obtained from its quality control surveys. Data from these surveys show that few recipients work and suggest that many recipients would face serious obstacles to finding and holding jobs.

Data from the department's quality control surveys over the period from 1979 to 1991 are shown in table 3-5. The caseload has grown younger over time, as the percentage of children younger than age 6, and especially under age 3, has climbed. Women, whether married or unmarried, who rear very young children ordinarily find it much harder to work than do women who are childless or whose children are 6 years old or older.

The educational attainment of AFDC mothers, though improving, remains low. Part of the lack of educational attainment can be explained by the extreme youth of many AFDC mothers. About 8 percent are under age 20 and nearly a quarter are between 20 and 24. Even so, the percentage of AFDC mothers with some college education is remarkably low. In 1991 only 12 percent reported one or more years of college, whereas slightly more than half of all women aged 25-34 have attended at least a year of college.

Less than 8 percent of the cases included in the quality control survey show evidence of current wage income. Some mothers who report no earnings to AFDC may nonetheless earn unreported wages or receive irregular labor income that goes

---

*This section was written by Gary Burtless.

unreported. In addition, many women who initially file for AFDC benefits have earned wages in the recent past. Over 60 percent of first-time claimants for welfare report work experience within the year before filing for AFDC.[63] In the mid-1980s, almost three-quarters of the typical welfare caseload reported *some* employment experience within the past five years.[64] Most available evidence suggests, however, that a majority of single women who are long-term recipients of AFDC do not work and do not have recent work experience. In the GAIN experiments in Alameda and Los Angeles Counties, California, for example, only 17 to 24 percent of the long-term AFDC recipients enrolled in the experiments reported any work experience within two years prior to their entry into the GAIN program.[65] Most of these long-term recipients had received AFDC continuously for at least three years at the time they entered GAIN.

Although there is no definitive study of the labor market experience of single women after they enter the AFDC rolls, most studies suggest that a substantial minority of AFDC mothers may become employed only after very lengthy periods without work, even if they are enrolled in a special training or job placement program. Daniel Friedlander and Gary Burtless examined the long-term effects of four welfare-to-work experiments conducted during the 1980s. In the fifth year after women were enrolled in these experiments, the employment rate averaged 38 percent among women who had been enrolled in the experimental welfare-to-work programs and 36 percent among women who had been enrolled in the control group.[66] Among women enrolled in the six-county GAIN experiment in California, only 40 percent held jobs at any time during the third year after enrollment. In the GAIN control group, only 34 percent of women in the control group held a job sometime during the third year after enrollment in the GAIN program began.[67] Employment rates were even more dismal in Alameda and Los Angeles Counties, where enrollment into GAIN was offered primarily to women who had continuously collected AFDC for several years. The findings from these experiments suggest extraordinary efforts will be needed to boost the employment rates of single AFDC mothers to rates that are typical among American mothers more generally. For purposes of comparison, about 63 percent of American women who have children under age 18 are employed; 43 percent of never-married mothers are employed; and 67 percent of widowed, divorced, and separated mothers with children under 18 hold jobs.[68]

Realistic Expectations about Employment

A minority of welfare recipients can be expected to leave the AFDC rolls within one year or less after entering the rolls. Many of them will leave welfare to take jobs, while others will leave AFDC because of a change in family composition or some other change that affects their continued eligibility for welfare. Women who remain dependent on welfare for longer periods may face a variety of obstacles to finding and holding a job. Many people who are sympathetic to the plight of poor single mothers view these obstacles as insurmountable "barriers" to employment. This viewpoint is unrealistic. Only a minority — probably a small one — of single mothers are prevented from working as a result of a supposed "barrier" to employment. It is more realistic to think about the various costs of entering employment. If society as a whole or single mothers themselves are willing to pay these costs, work should be considered a practical option for the great majority of mothers who receive AFDC. The problem, of course, is that mothers may be unwilling to bear these costs if the reward they receive from working is small. Since most welfare recipients do not have the skills that equip them to hold highly paid jobs, even a relatively minor cost of employment — such as a $3-a-day bus fare — may seem to constitute an formidable barrier to employment.

Welfare recipients face four kinds of obstacles to holding and keeping a job: work-limiting health conditions, deficiencies in education and basic skills, child care responsibilities, and transportation. Zill and others estimate that about 10 percent of AFDC recipients have health conditions that prevent them from working, while another 4 percent may have serious psychological problems.[69] It is unrealistic to expect that single mothers with serious physical or psychological problems are good candidates for full-time or even part-time jobs.

The educational and skill deficiencies of AFDC recipients restrict access to most well-paying occupations, but they do not preclude employment altogether. An unskilled welfare recipient, if she is able-bodied and moderately resourceful, can almost certainly find an employer willing to offer her a job if she is willing to accept a low enough wage and an inexpensive package of fringe benefits. In many urban labor markets, for example, jobless workers with few qualifications apply to temporary employment agencies for short-term work. Although the employment is uncertain and irregular, workers who are diligent and persistent can usually obtain at least occasional temporary work assignments and can often find permanent employment if their job performance impresses a manager who has provided a short-term assignment. Other job opportunities for less qualified workers can be found in low-wage retailing, cleaning services, agriculture, some manual labor, and informal child care. With relatively little training, less educated women can work as home health aides.

None of these job opportunities offers promising prospects for a good income or long-term advancement. It is important to recognize, however, that job opportunities exist for applicants who are willing to accept them, a fact confirmed by the job-finding success of unskilled immigrants. Many immigrants enter the United States suffering even worse disadvantages than those of long-term welfare recipients. Immigrants often have less schooling than most welfare recipients, and many of them cannot speak English. Immigrants who illegally reside in the United States are not eligible to collect income transfers, except emergency medical aid, so they must rely on their own earnings in order to survive. The great majority find jobs, and some unskilled immigrants eventually prosper.

It is less certain that unskilled AFDC recipients could find poorly paid jobs if hundreds of thousands or even millions of them were forced to find jobs within a one- or two-year period. If half of the 4 million adults who currently receive AFDC were removed from the welfare rolls, 2 million additional unskilled workers would flood the labor market looking for jobs. Though employers would eventually create enough unskilled positions to employ most of these job seekers, it is unrealistic to expect that new jobs would be created immediately. Most of the former AFDC recipients would face a lengthy wait before finding a job. In the long run, however, the skill deficiencies of AFDC recipients do not constitute an insurmountable barrier to employment.

The child care responsibilities of some recipients constitute a more serious long-term obstacle to work. Lack of child care is frequently cited as a reason for nonwork or for nonparticipation in a work-oriented activity, such as job training. This excuse is persuasive for single mothers with infants or children who have serious health problems that require an adult's constant care. It is less persuasive in a large majority of cases. Many single mothers can rely on parents, siblings, friends, or sexual partners to help care for their children when they are at work. Less fortunate are single mothers who are socially isolated and hence receive little help from their family and friends. These mothers must depend on subsidized child care or child care that is available in the market.

Unfortunately, there is little agreement among experts on the percentage of single mothers who must rely on expensive market-provided child care in order to work. If high-quality, generously subsidized care is available, many mothers will use such care in preference to informal arrangements. Even in those circumstances, however, many mothers prefer informal arrangements because they are much more convenient. If subsidized care is unavailable, most single mothers will be forced to rely on informal care provided by family, friends, or neighbors.

Transportation can represent a serious barrier to employment for single mothers who live in isolated areas, such as the countryside or rural towns. Even in these areas, however, many poor families have access to a car. For the three-quarters of welfare recipients who live in metropolitan areas, transportation represents a smaller obstacle to work. Job seekers can use public transportation to find jobs, and mothers who find jobs can often afford to buy an inexpensive car if public transportation turns out to be very inconvenient.

Summary

Taking into account the practical obstacles to work faced by most single mothers, it is not unreasonable to expect that at least three-quarters of current welfare recipients could contribute to their own support through wage earnings. Nearly all except those with very young children could be expected to work in full-time jobs. In many cases, AFDC recipients' work experience will turn out to be intermittent. The U.S. labor market offers few steady jobs to workers who have a serious deficit in skills. Whether it is sensible, humane, or cost-effective to force three-quarters of welfare recipients to find work remains an open question.

Table 3-5. Characteristics of AFDC Caseload, 1979-1991

Percent

Characteristic	1979	1986	1991
Ages of children			
Under 3	18.9	21.0	24.8
3 to 5	17.5	21.1	21.4
6 to 11	33.0	32.4	32.6
12 and over	29.8	24.3	21.4
Education of mother			
8th grade or less*	18.2	11.9	11.2
1-3 years high school*	39.8	35.5	35.1
4 years high school*	36.0	42.9	40.7
Some college*	5.2	8.4	12.2
College graduate*	0.8	1.2	0.8
Unknown	47.8	59.7	49.9
Mother's employment status			
Full-time job	8.7	1.6	2.2
Part-time job	5.4	4.2	4.2
Cases with reported earnings	12.8	7.5	7.9

*Percentage distribution among mothers whose educational attainment is known.
Source: Committee on Ways and Means, *1993 Green Book*, pp. 696-97.

What are the Effects of Work and Training Requirements on AFDC Recipients with Very Young Children?*

Discussion of welfare reform in the late 1980s and early 1990s often focused on the types of work-oriented programs that should be offered to AFDC recipients and kinds of recipients who should be obliged to participate in such programs. The programs offered to welfare recipients ranged from inexpensive interventions, such as loosely monitored job search, to such costly interventions as public service employment and long-term training. Policymakers and analysts have offered an equally wide range of proposals regarding the percentage of the AFDC recipients who should be subject to mandatory participation in work and training programs. Many observers think it makes sense to excuse single mothers who have children under age 6, who are usually too young to attend school. Others would require nearly all single mothers, including those with very young children, to find a job or participate at least part time in a work or training program.

During the 1980s a number of states tested a variety of new methods of training recipients and helping them find new or better jobs. Some of these programs were voluntary, but many were mandatory for at least some classes of AFDC recipients. The monthly benefits of recipients who did not participate in a mandated work program could be reduced or even eliminated. In a few places, policymakers attempted to force mothers with preschool children to participate in work-oriented activities.

Some states used classical experiments to assess the effectiveness of their new policies. The classical experimental method depends on random assignment in order to measure whether a new policy is more effective than the policy it replaces. Some people, selected at random, were enrolled in the new program, while other welfare recipients continued to collect welfare under the old rules. The success of the new policy was measured by comparing the experiences of the two groups. Since both were chosen at random, the difference in the subsequent experiences of the two groups was almost certainly due to the difference in the treatments they received. Policymakers could be confident that the new policy caused the difference in experiences, and they could ordinarily measure the exact difference in experiences with precision.

The experimental method also permits observation of the effects of the new policies on subgroups in the population initially enrolled. For example, analysts sometimes attempted to determine whether a new state policy was more effective in helping welfare recipients with older children or those with very young children. I examine below the findings from some of the welfare-to-work experiments that offer

*This section was written by Gary Burtless.

evidence on this issue. All of the experiments were evaluated by the Manpower Demonstration Research Corporation (MDRC).

The Arkansas WORK Program. The Arkansas Department of Human Services began operating the WORK program for single heads of AFDC families in 1982. Arkansas officials designed a fixed sequence of required activities for single mothers who were enrolled in the treatment group. Mothers were initially assigned to a two-week group job search (job club) program, which was followed by two months of individual job search. Women who remained unemployed after the second phase of the treatment were assigned to an unpaid community work experience position for up to twelve weeks. When this third phase was completed, jobless participants could be reassigned to one of the first two activities or occasionally to a new one.[70]

The state received a federal waiver to make the WORK program mandatory for mothers whose youngest child was 3 or older. At that time, most states imposed a work or training obligation on mothers whose youngest child was at least six years old. In two Arkansas counties, over half of enrolled mothers had children who were 3 to 5 years old. This was a large enough proportion of the sample to permit analysts to compare the effects of the WORK program on mothers with very young children and mothers whose youngest child was at least 6 years old.

Perhaps surprisingly, researchers could find little difference in the effectiveness of the WORK program for mothers with very young and older children. Among new applicants to welfare, the program helped increase the employment rate of mothers with children aged 3 to 5 by about 5 percentage points in the third calendar quarter after mothers were enrolled. If anything, the program probably had a smaller effect on the employment rate of AFDC applicants without very young children. Among mothers who were receiving AFDC at the time they were enrolled in the WORK program, the program may have boosted employment rates by 4 to 6 percentage points. There was no statistically significant difference between the effect observed on mothers with and without very young children.

The California GAIN Program. California's Greater Avenues for Independence (GAIN) program is the nation's largest welfare-to-work program. Begun in 1986, the program has historically emphasized mandatory basic education for AFDC recipients who lack a high school diploma or basic skills in reading, mathematics, or the English language. Basic educational services may be provided immediately before or immediately after a required period of intensive job search. A great deal of flexibility is offered to counties in establishing their own models of job placement and basic education. California officials selected six counties for inclusion in a randomized field trial of the GAIN program.[71]

In most California counties, mandatory participation in GAIN was initially restricted to mothers whose youngest child was at least 6 years old. In three of the counties included in the experiment, a supplementary sample was also enrolled that included mothers whose youngest child was 3 to 5 years old. These mothers were required to participate in mandatory GAIN activities in order to maintain their eligibility for full AFDC benefits.

As in the Arkansas study, analysts could find little evidence that the impact of the welfare-to-work program was significantly affected by the age of the mother's youngest child. In Riverside County, which achieved the largest earnings gains and AFDC benefit reductions of any of the six counties, the impacts of the GAIN program were approximately as large for the supplementary sample that included mothers with children under 6 as they were in the main analysis sample. The other two counties that enrolled small supplementary samples did not achieve very large initial effects in their main samples. They did not achieve very large effects in their supplementary samples, either. Thus neither the main sample, which excluded women with children under age 6, nor the supplementary sample, which included women with children under 6, realized substantial gains in earnings or reductions in AFDC payments. On balance, MDRC's analysts concluded that "local operators who can run programs that achieve impacts for other groups can also run programs that achieve impacts for the new (JOBS) mandatory group [which includes mothers with children under age six]."[72]

Florida's Project Independence. The state of Florida introduced a welfare-to-work program known as Project Independence in 1987.[73] The program emphasized immediate entry into the work force for most AFDC recipients. Furthermore, the basic program model required ongoing participation in a work-related activity for most mandatory participants, including single mothers with children as young as age 3. Except for the relatively small proportion of AFDC applicants and recipients who were exempt from participating, welfare recipients were required to attend an orientation session where Project Independence participants were divided into two service tracks.

Participants who were deemed to be "job ready" were initially assigned to a two-week period of individual job search. During this period they were asked to file job applications with at least twelve potential employers. Women failing to find a job were required to participate in a job club, where they were taught how to search for work, prepare a résumé, and present themselves in job interviews. After searching for an additional three weeks, women who did not find jobs received a formal job assessment and were asked to develop an employability plan, which could lead to education or training in local education and training institutions.

Project Independence participants who were initially found to be unprepared for work received a formal job assessment much earlier. They were then assigned to a basic education or training activity. The project initially provided a variety of support services, including child care, tuition assistance, transportation, work tools, and uniforms. Beginning in early 1991, public spending constraints forced project administrators to scale back financing for support services, especially child care. Mandatory participants in Project Independence could be excused from their participation obligation if necessary support services were unavailable. This limitation had an important effect on women who were most likely to need child care services, including mothers with very young children.

Initially, however, women with preschool children participated in Project Independence at about the same rate as mothers whose youngest child was 6 years old or older. Three-quarters of women in both groups attended the orientation session, and the majority of women who attended the orientation participated in at least one follow-up activity. After January 1991, however, the participation rates of women with young children fell in comparison with those of women whose youngest child was at least 6. If mothers are exempted from participating when child care services are unavailable, mothers with very young children will be less likely to participate in a welfare-to-work program in an environment of limited access to subsidized child care.

The initial findings from Project Independence suggested that Florida's welfare-to-work strategy was about as successful for mothers with very young children as it was for other mothers. During the first year after enrollment in the project, about 52 percent of mothers with young children in the control group found jobs, while 53 percent of control group mothers with older children found employment. Mothers assigned to the Project Independence treatment achieved first-year employment rates that were 3 to 4 percentage points higher than the control group's. The employment increase was almost the same among women with children under 6 as it was among women whose youngest child was at least 6 years old. AFDC dependency rates and average AFDC benefits were reduced as a result of mothers' participation in Project Independence, and the amount of AFDC reduction was quite similar for mothers with younger and older children. Earnings gains were larger for mothers with older children than for mothers with younger children, however: mothers whose youngest child was at least 6 enjoyed first-year earnings increases of $280 (11.2 percent of the control group mean), while mothers with younger children obtained earnings gains of just $74 (3.4 percent).[74]

It appears, however, that the employment and earnings gains of mothers with young children almost disappeared when child care services were scaled back. Among women whose youngest child was at least 6, the employment and earnings improvements continued (and, indeed, even improved) after access to child care services was restricted. This pattern of results suggests that at least limited subsidized child care must be available if mothers with younger children are obligated to participate in a work or training program.

All three experiments that have imposed mandatory work or training obligations on mothers with very young children provide evidence that such obligations can be about as successful for these mothers as they are for mothers with older children. The results from one experiment, Project Independence in Florida, show that this conclusion may be sensitive to program rules that exempt mothers from participating if no suitable child care can be found. Florida permitted exemptions from its standard work and training requirement in the case of mothers where no suitable child care arrangements could be made. This exemption had little effect when the state had modest funds to provide child care services to women who needed them. It made a larger difference after January 1991, when state budget constraints made it difficult to finance child care services for all mothers who needed them. Not surprisingly, the effect of the funding cutback was greatest on mothers with the youngest children.

What Would Happen If Time Limits Were Put on Cash AFDC Benefits, Followed By a Strongly Enforced Work Requirement?[*]

Proposals for putting time limits on welfare have taken two different forms. One form, proposed by economist (and former HHS assistant secretary) David T. Ellwood, involves turning cash welfare benefits into a transitional program. After a fixed period, recipients would be expected to work in public-service, nonprofit, or subsidized private-sector jobs if they could not find regular employment in the private sector.[75] "Hard time limits," the other form, would involve an end to all income support without a work guarantee.

Both types of time limits have been proposed in the current round of welfare reform. The Clinton administration's proposed 1994 Work and Responsibility Act included a phased-in work obligation after two years, with some exemptions and deferrals. It did not include hard time limits.

Republican proposals in the 104th Congress have focused primarily on hard time limits for use of federal family assistance block grant funds to aid recipients. Both the House-passed welfare reform bill and the Senate bill sponsored by Senate Majority Leader Robert Dole prohibit the use of federal family assistance block grant funds to pay benefits to individuals for a total of more than sixty months, regardless of the length of time between spells on welfare. Both bills allow states to exempt a small portion of their caseloads from such limits.[76] States could use their own funds to provide benefits for a longer period, but the financial pressures against doing so will be very strong. Moreover, states could provide benefits for a shorter period if they so desired.

---

[*]This section was written by Rebecca M. Blank.

The first type of time limits — requiring women to find a job and work a minimum number of hours in order to retain any eligibility for AFDC benefits after they have received cash assistance for a certain length of time — typically assumes that most women will find jobs in the private-sector, but many proposals require women who are unable to find work in the private sector to accept placement in some form of public sector employment.

If "work requirements" means that women must actually work a set number of hours in the private sector, a substantial number of women will have difficulty finding such a job. In 1993 the unemployment rate for female high school dropouts was 14 percent and was much higher for African American women and women in urban ghetto neighborhoods.[77] In addition, experience with existing welfare-to-work programs indicates that many jobs found by AFDC recipients are of short duration. Either the job itself ends, or problems in women's lives (sick children, inadequate transportation to work, family crises) cause them to quit or be fired.

One way around these problems is to expand "work requirements" to include either employment or active job search, thus allowing those without current employment to fulfill their work requirement by participating in job search and placement activities. This is what many state welfare-to-work programs already require. It is important to realize that *many* women will spend a substantial amount of time in job search activities and will return to those activities in between short spells of employment.

If "work requirements" means public-sector employment, this solves the problem of job unavailability and instability but creates significant public-sector management challenges. Running an effective and useful public-sector employment program is neither inexpensive nor easy. The nation's most recent experience with this was the Comprehensive Employment and Training Act (CETA), which operated between 1973 and 1983 and provided short-term jobs for a range of less-skilled workers. These jobs were largely located in public-sector and nonprofit agencies. Evaluations of CETA indicated that some increases in private-sector employment occurred among people who were placed in short (typically six-month) public-sector jobs. But there were ongoing management problems with CETA jobs. Local public unions often objected to these programs, fearing that agencies substituted subsidized workers for existing workers. Many workers received little skill enhancement from their CETA jobs.

Any public-sector placement program for AFDC women will not want to provide long-term placements, but will instead want to cycle women back into private-sector job search and placement programs on a regular basis. Thus problems of private-sector job availability will continue to exist in these programs as well.

It is worth noting that longer-term welfare recipients are the least prepared to work. They have less education, less work experience, and more and younger children; live in poorer neighborhoods, and are more likely to have health problems. While strong time limits, followed by job search, placement, and public-sector employment programs, will surely encourage more women to enter the labor market and to work more than they have in the past, it cannot be assumed that a high percentage of these women will become economically self-sufficient. In fact, existing welfare-to-work programs, while increasing employment and earnings, rarely allow participants to escape poverty.

Finally, a last issue of concern about time limits and work requirements is the extent to which exemptions to time limits might be available. Experience with work requirements for AFDC women indicates that there are some long-term AFDC recipients who are not employable, at least in the short run. These women may have very small children, health problems of their own or among other family members, behavioral problems, substance abuse problems, or a variety of family problems. Time-limit proposals must face the difficult fact that some AFDC participants, although representing quite a small share of the overall AFDC population, are probably not employable and will not be able to meet work requirements. Although program designers may be willing to cut these women off from benefits, it is not so easy to cut off their children.

What Would Happen If Time Limits Were Put on Cash Benefits Without a Work Guarantee?[*]

Proposals to eliminate all benefits to AFDC recipients after a specified time limit — "hard time limits" — will run into a variety of problems. First, not all women who seek work will be able to find work. Particularly among less-skilled workers, unemployment rates remain high even in times of economic expansion — especially, as noted earlier, among African American women and women in urban ghetto neighborhoods. If substantially more less-skilled women were thrown into the labor market in the short term, these unemployment rates could rise to even higher levels, at least temporarily.

Second, even among those who find work, many will be unemployed again in the near future. Research that tracks women who leave AFDC for work has emphasized the temporary nature of employment for many of these women, particularly when they first enter the labor market. In part, many available jobs are temporary or are at risk of being eliminated if business is bad. In addition, women who have primary child care duties often are fired when they miss a few days' work or

---

[*]This section was written by Rebecca M. Blank.

arrive late due to children's illnesses or other family problems. Many long-term AFDC recipients have little work experience, may not have good work discipline habits, and face other serious labor market disadvantages. LaDonna Pavetti has estimated that about three-quarters of the AFDC caseload at any given time would surpass a sixty-month time limit.[78]

As a result, few AFDC women are likely to be able to fully replace their AFDC benefits through employment. In fact, there is good evidence of this as a result of the AFDC eligibility changes implemented in 1981 and 1982 under President Reagan. About 12 percent of AFDC recipients became ineligible as a result of tightened eligibility in those years. These were predominantly women who had received only limited benefits; many of them were working as well as receiving some AFDC benefits. In short, this group was the *most advantaged* among AFDC recipients in terms of skills and work experience. A variety of studies all came to the same conclusion, summarized in a report from the General Accounting Office, which concluded that those women terminated from the AFDC program typically had monthly incomes 12 to 26 percent lower one and one-half to two years after the program change, "even though many worked full-time and increased their earnings during this period."[79] Recall that these women were the most prepared to work among existing AFDC recipients. Certainly, longer-term AFDC recipients will face even greater problems replacing AFDC income. Evidence from the termination of the General Assistance (GA) program in Michigan in 1991 found that only 28 percent of high school dropouts — and 46 percent of high school graduates — were employed two years after the GA program was terminated.[80]

It is likely that the great majority of longer-term AFDC recipients will end up poorer if AFDC benefits are terminated. Undoubtedly, terminating benefits will generate more work and employment among women and more earnings. Some of this will be in mainstream jobs and some will be in the underground economy. But the evidence indicates that few women will be able to replace their lost AFDC support through employment earnings. Women will work more but will have less income.

They will deal with this in a variety of ways. More women will move in with relatives, friends, or boyfriends. In some cases this will relieve economic problems; in other cases it may make them worse. Problems of overcrowding among poor families have been decreasing over time in this country, but this may be reversed if benefits are eliminated for many poor families. As noted in an earlier section of this chapter, researchers are discovering disturbingly high rates of past domestic and sexual abuse among AFDC recipients. Pushing women back into shared living arrangements may also increase this problem.

In the long run, substantial benefit cutoffs may also have feedback effects on pregnancy rates, divorce and marriage rates, and abortion rates. Given virtually no past experience with eliminating AFDC benefits for long-term users, it is hard to predict what the magnitude of these effects will be. Existing research suggests these effects are not large, but this research is based on more limited benefit changes, not on complete benefit cutoffs.

In addition, benefit termination will create a host of social problems in other areas. Homelessness among women and children will rise, and children may be under pressure to leave school early and earn income. Again, it is hard to predict the size of these effects. But the potential social costs of these changes must be weighed against any budget reductions occurring because of AFDC benefit cutoffs.

How Much Variation Is There In the Current System of AFDC Benefits and Eligibility?*

AFDC benefits vary dramatically among the states. Among the lower forty-eight states, for example, Connecticut paid an average of almost $2,400 annually per AFDC recipient in 1993, while Mississippi granted just $504 (table 3-6).[81] Ten states paid more than $2,000 per recipient on average in 1993; eight states paid less than $1,000. Annual AFDC benefits per recipient in the average state were about $1,570.

States differ even more in their own contributions to AFDC payments. Connecticut spent about $1,200 annually of its own funds on each AFDC recipient (with the federal government picking up the other $1200). In contrast, Mississippi spent only $102 per recipient (while the federal government paid $398, almost 79 percent of the total).[82]

Eligibility criteria also vary from state to state. There is no simple way to compare these criteria in order to identify the states where it is easier to obtain AFDC benefits.[83] In the 1980s, however, it was easier in general to gain access to the welfare rolls in states offering more generous AFDC benefits.[84]

The range in AFDC benefits among the states has remained large over the past twenty-five years. Maximum AFDC benefits for a three-person family were about five times higher in Connecticut than in Mississippi in 1970; by 1994 Connecticut's maximum benefits were almost six times higher. Still, real AFDC benefits declined sharply during this period. In 1994 maximum AFDC benefits in the median state were almost 50 percent lower than they were in 1970.[85]

Both the real decline in AFDC benefit levels over time and interstate differentials in AFDC benefits are partially reduced by the effects of Food Stamp

---

*This section was written by Mark C. Rom.

benefits, however. Food Stamp benefits increase as cash benefits decline, and are indexed automatically for inflation. The maximum combined monthly benefit of AFDC plus Food Stamps for a single-parent family of three persons in Connecticut in January 1994 was $872, slightly more than twice Mississippi's $415. The median state value was $661.[86]

Table 3-6. Annual AFDC Benefits per Recipient, by State, 1993

State	Benefit (dollars)	Rank	State	Benefit (dollars)	Rank
Alabama	684	48	Montana	1416	26
Alaska	3,036	1	Nebraska	1,356	29
Arizona	1,368	28	Nevada	1,248	34
Arkansas	828	45	New Hampshire	1,896	11
California	2,376	4	New Jersey	1,536	18
Colorado	1,332	31	New Mexico	1,248	36
Connecticut	2,388	3	New York	2,220	7
Delaware	1,428	23	North Carolina	1,056	42
District of Columbia	1,692	16	North Dakota	1,524	19
Florida	1,164	38	Ohio	1,368	27
Georgia	1,080	39	Oklahoma	1,248	33
Hawaii	2,568	2	Oregon	1,716	15
Idaho	1,344	30	Pennsylvania	1,512	20
Illinois	1,284	32	Rhode Island	2,172	8
Indiana	1,056	41	South Carolina	804	46
Iowa	1,620	17	South Dakota	1,248	35
Kansas	1,428	25	Tennessee	708	47
Kentucky	936	44	Texas	684	49
Louisiana	672	50	Utah	1,488	21
Maine	1,740	13	Vermont	2,304	6
Maryland	1,428	24	Virginia	1,188	37
Massachusetts	2,304	5	Washington	2,100	9
Michigan	1728	14	West Virginia	1,020	43
Minnesota	2004	10	Wisconsin	1,860	12
Mississippi	504	51	Wyoming	1,452	22
Missouri	1,080	40			

Source: Author's calculations from data in *1994 Green Book*, pp. 391-92.

Do High-Benefit States Act as "Welfare Magnets"?*

A state that offers high AFDC benefits or permissive eligibility criteria *could* become a "welfare magnet" *if* individuals chose to live there to take advantage of the state's generosity. It is clear that *if* a state's benefits were high enough and its eligibility loose enough it would become a welfare magnet.

Yet scholars have been unable to prove whether welfare magnets actually exist. Several studies have found that states offering generous welfare benefits do have a slightly magnetic effect.[87] Other studies have disputed these results.[88] There are two main reasons for this disagreement. First, it is devilishly difficult to test whether welfare influences migration.[89] As it turns out, poor people decide where to live for a complex mix of personal and economic reasons, so it is not easy to determine how important welfare is in that decision. Second, the magnetic effect, if any, of the existing welfare programs must be small. If welfare magnets were strong and stable, the research conclusions would be more consistent.

Politicians in high-benefit states are convinced nonetheless that they face a real problem. Yet the states cannot bar new residents from receiving AFDC.[90] States are trying, however, to take other steps to discourage new residents from obtaining welfare. Wisconsin and California have received waivers from the federal government to create "two-tier" welfare systems in which new residents on AFDC would receive the same level of benefits as they did in their former state for up to one year.[91] It is not clear whether these two-tier systems will pass legal scrutiny.[92] The House-passed welfare reform bill would explicitly allow any state to treat newly arriving AFDC recipients under the eligibility and benefit rules of their former state for up to twelve months after their arrival.[93] Some states (California, for example) are simply cutting AFDC benefits to make their states less attractive to the poor from other states.

What Would be the Effects on Recipients and Expenditures of Restrictions on AFDC Benefits to Recipients Who Migrate from One State to Another?*

Two-tier systems will have almost no effect on state budgets, welfare rolls, or recipient behavior, although they will increase the administrative complexity of AFDC. A state's spending on AFDC benefits would almost certainly decline by less than 1 percent in even the strongest welfare magnets.[94] Nationwide, these policies

---

*This section was written by Mark C. Rom.

*This section was written by Mark C. Rom.

would have almost no effect on the number of welfare recipients.[95] Two-tier benefit systems might slightly decrease the mobility of those on AFDC.[96] Still, potential recipients might have some incentive to move to high-benefit states to obtain welfare payments; they would simply have to wait one year after arrival to receive them. States that adopt two-tier systems would face the administrative burden of collecting and verifying additional information (regarding previous residency and welfare payments) from welfare applicants.

More serious welfare magnet effects could occur, however, if states are allowed to set "hard time limits" (neither cash benefits nor a job guarantee) at a duration of their own choosing. In this case, the differential is not between higher and lower benefits, but between benefits or a job and nothing at all. Significant migration could occur from low-duration to high-duration states as recipients approached the end of their eligibility (or approached one year of remaining eligibility in their home state if states were allowed to apply rules of the home state to immigrants for one year). The eventual outcome would likely be a race to the bottom in the duration of hard time limits, with most or all states shortening those limits as they sought to avoid becoming welfare magnets. To avoid such an eventuality, it is essential that if hard time limits are enacted, they be set at a uniform minimum level for all states.

4. Administrative Capacity and Welfare Reform

*Evelyn Z. Brodkin**

Welfare reform legislation currently under consideration in Congress represents a marked departure from the arrangement of shared federal-state responsibilities developed over the past fifty years. That arrangement has been distinguished by increasing federal fiscal support for state welfare programs coupled with increasing federal regulation and oversight of state practice. Welfare bills approved by the House and by the Senate Finance Committee would reverse this trend. Generally, they increase state discretion in setting and administering welfare policy while decreasing federal fiscal support.

However, specific features of reform legislation present a more complicated picture. The bills combine welfare benefits and job programs into a block grant and freeze federal funding at 1994 levels. They also impose new mandates that more than double the proportion of welfare recipients states must move into work or training within the next eight years. States that fail to meet these requirements will be subject to fiscal penalties. Consequently, states gain greater flexibility in some areas of policy and administration, but they lose the flexibility of current funding mechanisms that guarantee federal support for more than half the cost of state welfare benefits. In addition, states risk funding losses if they cannot meet tough new work requirements.[97]

Although state administrative capacity has always been important to the success or failure of welfare policy, these new measures dramatically raise the stakes for both states and poor families. Unless states become far more efficient and effective in supporting transitions from welfare to work, frozen funding and fiscal penalties will leave them with less federal support to sustain both their work and benefits programs.[98] If state performance falls short, they will face the unattractive options of either increasing state welfare funding or simply cutting assistance to needy families.

---

*The author would like to acknowledge valuable comments on drafts of this chapter from Mark Greenberg, Irene Lurie, Jim Riccio, and Michael Sosin.

Given the stakes, it is striking that little attention has been devoted in the current welfare debate to understanding whether states have the capacity to meet these new responsibilities or what they will need — beyond flexibility — in order to carry them out. Yet experience cautions against expecting that complex problems of welfare administration can be made to disappear simply by turning them over to the states.

This chapter reviews what is known about state capacity to administer policies that promote transitions from welfare to work. It discusses lessons learned from state experience, identifies problems proposed legislation may create, and suggests ways to address those problems and help states build the capacity to assume a greater welfare role.

Lessons from Prior Experience

Prior experience offers some indications about what states now have the capacity to do and what they may need in order to build their capacity. For example, evaluations of welfare-to-work programs demonstrate that states can help support transitions from welfare to work. At 1994 funding levels, states were able to meet requirements that they engage 15 percent of single parents in job activities, after exempting those who could not participate because of child care, health, or family problems. But preliminary HHS data indicate that forty states were unable to meet requirements that they serve 40 percent of two-parent households. Despite this mixed record, current proposals more than double these participation standards, requiring states to place in work activities 50 percent of single parents and 90 percent of household heads in two-parent families *without* exemptions for child care, health, or other problems.

Experience also shows that states have produced modest improvements in work hours and earnings for job program participants in a variety of experimental settings. But states have not been able to bring large numbers of families out of poverty through work alone, as reform legislation anticipates they can. Even one of the most successful programs studied (in Riverside, California) was able to increase by only 4.6 percent the proportion of recipients who both became employed and left welfare.[99]

Given the record to date, it takes an unwarranted leap of faith to assume that states have the capacity to serve more than double the current number of welfare recipients effectively and move them in unprecedented numbers into steady work — especially with federal aid frozen at 1994 levels. While the accomplishments of a few selected state agencies have been celebrated, less attention has been paid to the widely varied results achieved by welfare-to-work programs across the country.

Their record provides lessons about both the limits and the possibilities for improving state capacity to implement welfare reform.

The Limits of Model Programs

A handful of agencies have demonstrated exceptional, albeit still modest, success in operating welfare-to-work programs. On the surface, this may seem to indicate that other agencies can substantially improve their performance by emulating the formal models that have worked elsewhere. However, the situation is not that simple.

Program models that work well for one agency may fail to produce good results in others. In both the WIN demonstrations and the JOBS program, states have drawn from a similar menu of education, training, and job-search options in designing welfare-to-work programs. Yet results vary widely. Because agencies have used program elements in different proportions and for welfare recipients with diverse educational or work backgrounds, it has been difficult to fully assess why some have been more effective than others. This may seem to argue for giving states more flexibility to devise their own programs. However, without adequate knowledge about what works best under specific conditions, neither states nor the federal government can fully anticipate the consequences of their choices.

In fact, the notion of "model" programs may turn out to be deceptively simple. Generally, the term "model" refers to the types of job preparation and job finding activities offered (such as education, training and job search), the types and extensiveness of supportive services provided (for example, child care and transportation) and the incentives or penalties attached to program participation. However, the same service model, when implemented under different conditions or in different ways, may produce different effects. In experimental studies of California's GAIN program, the Manpower Demonstration Research Corporation (MDRC) found that counties implementing a similar program model produced substantially different results.

The picture becomes more complicated when one attempts to account for relatively similar results produced by programs using different approaches. For example, among the six programs MDRC studied in California, those in Riverside and Alameda differed most in their emphasis on job search versus education, provision of supportive services, and approaches to participation. Yet among certain subgroups, they produced comparably high improvements in earnings.[100] Specific factors such as types of services provided, the background of clients served, or economic conditions do not seem to fully explain varied program outcomes.

To replicate the success of exceptional programs, agencies will have to do more than simply adopt the same mix of formal program elements. They will have to develop the administrative capacity and methods of casework practice that enable them to manage programs effectively under varied and changing local conditions. However, the administrative and operational factors that enable agencies to run programs effectively are difficult to specify and even when specified may be hard to replicate.

For example, speculation about the sources of Riverside's singular results has turned up a variety of distinctive factors, including the efforts of staff job developers, management's unusual extent of control over personnel decisions, the absence of a large inner city population with high concentrations of poverty, the agency's relatively small size and nonurban location, its relationship to other county agencies providing welfare-to-work services, the strong political backing of the county's welfare director, and staff attitudes toward work. However, it is unknown which of these factors may be significant or to what extent. Nor is it known whether other agencies lacking some or all of these characteristics (some of which are beyond agency control) can duplicate Riverside's results.

In speculations about Riverside's results, one factor — the agency's purportedly "tough" attitude toward work — has received disproportionate attention, leading to suggestions that other agencies can become more effective by becoming "tougher." However, the simple depiction of Riverside as "tough" mischaracterizes a program that did more than exhort its participants or make demands on them. It provided a variety of education, training, and job development services, most of which have been associated with positive employment results elsewhere, including in agencies using different casework approaches. Researchers disagree about the effectiveness of "tough" or "supportive" casework practices, and competing claims cannot be validated on the basis of available evidence.[101] The benefits and hazards of alternative approaches require clearer specification and more systematic study before "best practice" models of casework can be devised.

States also need better information about how to build their capacity to operate programs effectively. National evaluations of the Job Opportunities and Basic Skills (JOBS) program and evaluations currently required for states receiving waivers are building knowledge about how to create better programs. But there is much more that we need to learn. This can best be accomplished by more careful testing and evaluations. Giving states unlimited authority to design their programs without making provision for testing or evaluation will set back efforts to help states learn from experience.

Big Cities' Problems

If welfare reform is to advance national goals, it must be effective in big cities with large numbers of poor families. But recent experience suggests that reform could founder in big cities, especially those experiencing tight funding and increasing poverty populations.

Factors particular to welfare administration in big cities are likely to make effective program operation more difficult. For one thing, the logistics of delivering a large program raise distinctive problems of coordination, monitoring, and case processing. The kinds of internal flexibility demonstrated in smaller agencies, where officials interact informally to resolve problems as they arise are often precluded when agencies are large. The formal arrangements necessary to organize and coordinate work on a large scale do not easily permit the fluid and informal problem solving that can improve effectiveness in smaller agencies.

Problems of coordination among large city agencies and conflicts between city and state agencies can also make program operation more difficult. A ten-state implementation study reported that "the existence of large bureaucracies complicated the process of sharing information and created turf problems, making interagency coordination more difficult than in the less urban sites."[102] Freeing states from federal regulation will not make cooperation any more likely and, as federal funding decreases, may even intensify competitiveness.

Even well-run programs may prove less effective in large cities than in smaller cities or nonurban areas, especially in cities that have a high percentage of poor adults needing assistance. Successful operation of welfare-to-work programs often depends on the availability of support for welfare recipients by other government programs that provide education, training, and job placement services. Urban agencies that serve a high proportion of welfare recipients may be more quickly overwhelmed by increased participation requirements than agencies in which welfare recipients comprise a relatively small share of their consumer demand.

Also, job placement may be especially difficult in areas with high-density poverty and low job growth. In those areas, local labor markets may become saturated as larger numbers of welfare recipients seek entry. Consequently, some big city agencies are likely to produce more modest effects than agencies operating under more favorable conditions.[103]

It is notable that the most highly evaluated programs have tended to be either in smaller cities and nonurban areas, or they have been operated on a small scale by private agencies. It is troubling that among the six programs subjected to a careful experimental test in California, the Los Angeles program demonstrated the lowest third year earnings and employment impacts.

Studies of programs in Los Angeles, New York, Chicago and Detroit indicate that difficulties associated with big city administration may be fairly common.[104] But, for various methodological reasons, evaluation studies do not permit an adequate assessment of the reasons for these differences. They do suggest that the particular features of urban program administration may limit what big city agencies can achieve.

Administrative Resource Constraints

Program effectiveness depends on agencies' capacity to perform a wide variety of tasks. Although administrative details are the stuff that Martin Anderson once warned "make people's eyes glaze over," it is these day-to-day activities that determine how well national policy goals will be translated into practice. As with other aspects of policy implementation, there is more to this process than good intentions.

If states are to increase participation in work, they will need to be able to pay for services that support transitions to work. The precise amount of money each state needs will depend on a variety of factors, many beyond direct agency control, including the size of its population in poverty, the severity of clients' needs, job opportunities available in the local economy, and the ability of a state to leverage "free" services from other agencies. In the past, welfare-to-work programs have been operated at a cost of anywhere from a few hundred dollars per participant (for job search-only programs) up to $16,000 per participant (for intensive supported work programs). As noted in chapter 3, program costs also depend on the trade-off states make between more expensive service strategies that lead to higher wages and the less expensive services that increase work hours but not wages.

Beyond the question of which service strategy to use, all welfare-to-work programs incur costs for basic services that enable participants to work, among them costs for transportation to work and work equipment (for example, uniforms or tools). The largest basic cost is for child care, an essential service for single parents whose children are at home either because they are too young for school or they are ill or on school holiday. States have always exempted single parents from work requirements when they lacked access to child care. The cost of assuring access limited efforts to increase participation in job-related activities from the WIN programs of the seventies to the JOBS programs of the nineties. Even if the child care guarantee were eliminated, there is no obvious way that states could substantially increase participation among single parents without putting young children at risk.

Although there is reason to be skeptical that greater effectiveness can be achieved by throwing money at a problem, so too is there reason to be skeptical that greater effectiveness can be achieved by reducing money available to deal with a problem. In at least one state, Florida, the earnings gains produced by its welfare-to-work program sharply deteriorated after the program suffered a major budget cut. Welfare recipients who entered the program in its scaled down form had no greater earnings than recipients who did not participate in the program.[105] If capped block grants produce the race to the bottom that most experts predict, funding for welfare-to-work programs could drop below the minimum threshold needed to operate them effectively.

If states are to support transitions to work, they will also need agency staff of sufficient size and skill to operate programs effectively. Although research has not clarified an optimal staff size for efficient program operation, it is evident that there are limits to what caseworkers can do well if caseload size, administrative tasks, or casework responsibilities become too burdensome. Lurie and Hagen found understaffing to be a common problem, constraining what caseworkers could do to help recipients find the best work and training opportunities, monitor their progress, respond to special problems, and attend to routine administrative tasks. Even when staff shortages were an acknowledged impediment to program performance, agency managers were rarely able to get state legislative approval to add staff, a situation that is likely to worsen under a block grant approach.[106]

Even if numbers of staff were adequate, the effectiveness of agency programs would be constrained by the capacity of staff to perform casework effectively. The skills and knowledge welfare-to-work caseworkers require are of a different order than those needed to perform the simpler administrative tasks of payment processing. Consider the types of judgements that caseworkers are routinely expected to make in assessing client needs, evaluating the best route to employment, matching clients with appropriate services, and judging progress and performance. To perform these tasks well, caseworkers need skills and training equivalent to that of human resources counselors, social workers, teachers, or others in related professions.[107]

However, most welfare agencies are staffed by nonprofessional caseworkers of varied ability and educational background; many are without college degrees. In agencies where managers have little or no control over personnel selection, staff appointments may be contingent on length of service with the welfare agency rather than qualifications particular to the position. National reforms that free state agencies from federal regulation do not change state civil service laws or other locally based restrictions on management authority. Nor do they provide additional financing to states that want to increase staff capacity through education or training. Agencies will need to invest in building staff capacity if they are to transform them into effective operators of welfare-to-work programs.

As in any organization, even skilled staff cannot be expected to do good work unless provided with resources commensurate with their tasks. Critics of welfare agency practice correctly point out that caseworkers cannot be expected to advance substantive policy goals when they are overly burdened with administrative tasks. Liberating caseworkers from some of these tasks frees one resource — time — for other purposes. However, time and skills are not the only resources caseworkers need.[108]

Regardless of their workload, skills, or philosophy, caseworkers are likely to be ineffective in moving welfare recipients into education, training, or employment unless they have access to an adequate supply of services and work opportunities. When asked what they need to be effective in promoting transitions to work, agency staff repeatedly ask for exactly what their clients have asked for: a supply of available jobs. They also ask for skilled job developers who can get access to those jobs.[109]

Without access to job information and opportunities, caseworkers can do little more to promote work than offer encouragement or exhortation. At worst, they can use their authority to put clients through meaningless procedural hoops or threaten them with sanctions for "noncompliance" with program regulations. Giving caseworkers increased authority without ensuring that they have adequate resources and skills to support transitions into work and out of poverty endangers both program effectiveness and accountability.

Accountability for Performance

Accountability in the provision of welfare and other public services has long been a vexing problem for managers, legislators, and analysts. Unlike other types of products, welfare services are not subject to market regulation because most consumers of welfare-to-work services are involuntary and cannot shop for the best products. Consequently, performance measurement, sometimes coupled with fiscal inducements or penalties, have become standard tools for achieving accountability in welfare delivery.

Unless carefully crafted, performance measures can distort agency practice in ways that undermine effectiveness. Agencies generally respond to performance measures, especially when they are linked to fiscal rewards or penalties. To meet measured aspects of performance — for participation, target group enrollment, or procedural accuracy, for instance — agencies invest time, attention, and material resources. However, dedicating resources to one set of objectives means that fewer resources will be available for the pursuit of others. The result is that unmeasured aspects of performance may suffer. For example, in response to the threat of financial penalties for erroneous overpayments to welfare recipients, states imposed an array of new procedures to reduce the risk of overpaying benefits. However, these procedures increased the risk of making underpayments and failing to provide benefits to eligible families, a trade-off between measured and unmeasured aspects of performance.

Although measured errors decreased, the goal of improved accuracy was poorly served.[110]

In welfare-to-work programs, performance measures that focus exclusively on quantity — numbers of participants — without attention to quality, place quality at risk. The risk to quality increases as participation quotas increase but resources do not. Participation quotas of various kinds have long been part of welfare-to-work legislation. In both the WIN and JOBS programs, Congress has employed quotas to hold states accountable for using federal funds to promote work. However, states' capacity to promote work varies depending on staff skills, funding for services, economic conditions, participant job qualifications, and so forth. Fixed, numerical quotas that do not take capacity into account create incentives for agencies to trade quality for quantity and to engage in strategic games to "meet the numbers." For example, they may stretch resource limits by providing inexpensive, low-quality services or placements, although these may be of little benefit to participants. Or, they may game the numbers by recruiting those participants most easily placed (creaming), by redefining participant needs to fit available service slots (slotting), or by exempting those recipients who are hardest to serve (exempting).[111]

Poorly designed requirements for moving recipients from welfare to work can create especially perverse consequences. In the past, caseworkers have responded to quotas (such as those in the House bill) for moving recipients into jobs by misusing their authority over clients to clear the rolls of participants they could not place. In one WIN demonstration program, overuse of sanctions for noncompliance eventually resulted in court intervention to stop these practices.[112] For these and other reasons, accountability and policy goals may be ill-served by performance measures emphasizing the number of participants in work and training.

Current Legislation: Problems and Options for Improvement

Current reform proposals have one thing in common with previous policy. Both rely on state welfare agencies for the achievement of national goals. Over the decades, federal dependence on state administration has been a source of continuing tension over how much money the federal government would provide, how much autonomy states would retain, and how to hold states accountable for their performance. These tensions are inherent in any arrangement in which the federal government supplies funds, but does not directly control policy delivery.

Congress has utilized two types of strategies to induce states to operate welfare programs in ways that will advance national goals. One strategy attempts to control state practice by mandating policy and performance requirements, penalizing states that fail to meet them. The other strategy attempts to encourage state progress toward national goals by providing additional resources and rewarding effective performance. Generally, policy has incorporated a mix of these two strategies. It asserts a congressional prerogative to set policy goals, but implicitly recognizes that unless states have the wherewithal to translate policy requirements into practice, simply mandating performance will be an empty gesture.

Changing the balance between these strategies by altering provisions for funding, incentives, and accountability, can influence state administration in complex and often unintended ways. No strategy offers a sure and simple way to ensure that states will move large numbers of families into work or out of poverty. But flaws in current legislative proposals that tilt the balance toward mandates and away from capacity-building are likely to have perverse consequences for state welfare administration and work at cross purposes with the stated hopes of reform. The remainder of this chapter discusses problems with current legislative proposals and options for improving them.

Problem: Proposed legislation increases requirements for what the states must do to move recipients from welfare to work, but decreases federal support for those efforts.

This mismatch between resources and requirements spells trouble for program quality and effectiveness. The House and Senate Finance Committee bills raise requirements for program participation and for transitions off welfare to levels well beyond anything achieved to date. State agencies will be responsible for nearly doubling the number of work program participants for whom they must conduct assessments, find work and training placements, monitor activities, and provide job search assistance. It is unlikely that states can manage these tasks with existing staff and fiscal resources without sacrificing accuracy or quality. If states are to meet new requirements, they will need more of the resources that, in many places, are already in short supply: skilled staff, day care, and training and job opportunities.

It is also unlikely that states will be able to increase administrative efficiency enough to transfer additional resources from benefits processing to job programs. Agencies will continue to have to perform complex determinations of welfare eligibility — determinations that will be made more complex if states are required to administer time limits, restrictions on childbearing, and complicated new rules for immigrants. The prospects for agencies acquiring increased state funding to add, upgrade, or train staff to respond to new responsibilities also seem remote. States would have more flexibility to allocate funds between benefits, work programs and administration. But that will only permit tradeoffs among these functions, not increase the resources to perform them.

Resource constraints may be felt most acutely in the provision of child care. Under all previous legislation, states that could not assure child care for single parents could not require them to participate in work or training. The House bill takes the unprecedented step of eliminating any guarantee of child care. The Senate Finance Committee bill has language requiring child care, but does not specify what states must provide or how the requirement will be enforced. Neither bill increases the federal commitment to help states pay for the additional child care needed to meet higher work participation requirements. When calculating compliance with participation quotas, states are prohibited from excluding as "unable to participate" parents without adequate child care.

The Congressional Budget Office estimates that for states to meet new work requirements — including the provision of day care for small children — at current rates of expenditure per participant will consume $10 billion of the $16.8 billion provided in the Senate Finance Committee bill for benefits and work programs combined. Without increasing the supply of resources to match new demands, it is unclear how states will be able to meet those requirements and still protect children needing day care.

The mismatch between resources and requirements also makes it doubtful that the progress made to date in developing welfare-to-work programs can be sustained. As in the production of any service or product, if welfare resources are reduced and production increased, the quality of the product can be expected to suffer. The only factors that could alter this equation would be a substantial growth in the availability of jobs for low-skilled workers or the development of a new technology that permits production of services at lower cost. Neither of these advances seems likely.

If states cannot do more with less, they will be faced with some unattractive options: increasing their own contributions substantially or choosing whether to cut welfare benefits, reduce work and training programs, or both. Most likely there will be a "race to the bottom" along two lanes: one for benefits, the other for services. If this occurs, funding for work programs may fall below the minimum threshold necessary to operate them effectively. Poor families face the greatest risk from ineffective welfare-to-work programs if states are unable or unwilling to provide income assistance to recipients that their job programs fail to help.

Options: Reduce the mismatch between resources and requirements that threatens state capacity to provide assistance and promote work effectively.

—Set more realistic participation requirements that take account of state capacity. If federal funding is frozen at 1994 levels, participation rates should be frozen at the same levels. If participation rates are set too high relative to state capacity, they undermine accountability by creating incentives for states either to produce work programs of little value or to ignore participation requirements. Alternatively, Congress could set targets for work program participation, but eliminate fiscal sanctions. This avoids imposing an unfunded mandate, increases state flexibility to respond to circumstances beyond their control, but still "sends a message" about participation.

—Require states to assure child care for single parents participating in work programs or exempt from requirements parents who do not have access to child care. Single parents who are unable to participate in work programs without child care should be excluded from participation rate calculations.

—If welfare programs are converted into a block grant and funding is frozen, pressures for a "race to the bottom" can be slowed by adding a maintenance of effort provision that requires states to sustain current funding levels. Such a provision would effectively produce a freeze on both state and federal welfare funding. It would not assure adequate state capacity to become more effective in promoting work and reducing poverty, but it would help avert a decline in that capacity.

—Maintain AFDC as an entitlement. Until states can demonstrate greater effectiveness in reducing the need for welfare, benefits for families in which parents are — if able — preparing for work, searching for work, or working at below poverty levels should be protected. Otherwise, recipients who participate in good faith in work programs that are ineffective will be unfairly penalized. Benefits for families in which parents are unable to work due to illness or other problems should also be secured.

Problem: Mechanisms to hold states accountable for effective performance toward policy goals are flawed and could do more harm than good.

The House bill and Senate Finance Committee bill rely heavily on participation rate requirements and fiscal penalties to induce state performance toward national goals. However, by increasing requirements without increasing state capacity to meet them, these measures are unlikely to advance those goals and may even work at cross purposes to them.

Increasing participation requirements beyond state service capacity creates perverse incentives to favor quantity over quality. States that want to maximize federal funding needed to sustain their welfare programs will want to avoid fiscal penalties. Paradoxically, that may mean increasing program participation beyond the numbers that can be served effectively. The Florida experience suggests that, beyond a certain threshold, work programs may simply force recipients through a series of meaningless activities that do not improve their employment prospects. Consequently, it is possible that the better states perform in meeting participation rates, the worse their programs may become.

These problems are exacerbated by flaws in the formula for measuring participation. First, in the House bill, states are credited with successfully promoting transitions to work if welfare recipients leave welfare *for any reason* (other than requirements of federal law), not only because they have found work that pays well enough to end their need for welfare. The danger in this feature is that it does not encourage agencies to become more effective in supporting transitions to work, but it does encourage them to find ways to push recipients off welfare by churning them in and out of temporary jobs, overusing sanctions for noncompliance with rules, or simply narrowing eligibility for assistance to include fewer poor families.

Second, as previously discussed, neither the House bill nor the Senate Finance Committee bill permits states to exempt single parents who lack access to adequate child care from its participation rate calculations. This, too, creates a paradox. If states provide child care funding adequate to meet increased participation rates, they will have much less money available to serve larger numbers of work program participants. If they ignore participation rates, they will face fiscal penalties, again reducing available funds.

Third, the formula does not protect either states or welfare recipients against circumstances beyond their control that effect their capacity to meet participation requirements. In calculating participation rates, states would not be permitted to exempt adults unable to work because of health or emotional problems, domestic abuse or homelessness. Even in Riverside, known for its emphasis on work, 48 percent of participants in the job program were deferred at some point. The largest number of deferrals, aside from those given to recipients already working part-time, were given in response to illness, family crises, and emotional or mental problems.[113]

Fourth, the participation rate formula makes no allowance for special circumstances beyond state control that make operation of welfare-to-work programs more difficult, including high concentrations of urban poverty, increasing poverty populations, and economic recessions. Using fiscal penalties to hold states accountable for aspects of performance that they cannot control will not encourage effective program operation or help states build the capacity to become more effective. Perversely, penalties may hit hardest those parts of the country facing the most difficult tasks.

Fifth, the House bill narrows the definition of work and training that "counts" toward participation. It eliminates from that definition some educational activities that have shown the greatest promise for reducing poverty over the long-term. It also precludes states from subtracting from participation calculations those welfare cases comprised only of children, where there is no adult receiving welfare and, therefore, bound by its requirements.

Options: Improve accountability by correcting provisions that are likely to have perverse consequences for state practice and could put children at risk.

—Reduce participation rates to more realistic levels, or use them as targets, but eliminate fiscal sanctions.

—If participation rates and sanctions are retained, eliminate provisions that permit states to count exits from welfare for reasons other than work as if they constituted successful transitions to work.

—Exempt from work requirements single parents who do not have access to adequate child care. Exclude those families when calculating state participation rates.

—Exempt from work requirements adults who are unable to work because of health or family problems. Exclude those families when calculating state participation rates. Also exclude from those calculations cases that do not include an adult recipient.

—Permit HHS to adjust participation rate requirements to take account of circumstances beyond state control that make those rates harder to meet in some areas of the country than others. Those circumstances include high concentrations of urban poverty, increases in the poverty population, and recession or high levels of unemployment.

—Eliminate House restrictions on the types of work preparation activities that count toward participation.

Problem: Opportunities to learn from experience may be lost, and innovation may be discouraged.

Giving states flexibility to fashion programs without creating mechanisms to learn from experience will leave states without the knowledge necessary to make better choices in the future. Under existing legislation, states receiving waivers to test alternative policy approaches have been required to evaluate program effects. Without these requirements, few states invest in systematic evaluations of policy impacts, instead collecting only the basic statistics that federal rules require. Increasing state flexibility without providing mechanisms to assess what works and what does not will leave both Congress and the states with inadequate information to assess the consequences of reform and learn from experience.

Even if evaluations are conducted, state flexibility may yield less knowledge from innovation than hoped, for three reasons. First, pending bills that reduce funding but increase participation requirements may make states more conservative in their approach to welfare policy. States may be less willing to attempt innovative programs if they risk fiscal penalties for attempts that do not work out. They could be more inclined to stick to conservative and low-cost approaches, and certainly would be discouraged from pursuing education and training strategies requiring up-front investments in pursuit of long-term payoffs.

Second, those states that do initiate innovations but encounter difficulties in their early stages may end them quickly in order to avoid fiscal penalties. If this occurs, opportunities to learn from trial and error and assess longer-term effects will be lost. Third, if states try to stay the course and weather fiscal penalties, it may become more difficult for them to operate their programs effectively. Consequently, it may not be possible to determine whether their innovations might have succeeded under more favorable operating conditions. Expecting individual states to assume too high a risk for innovation may inhibit the kinds of experimentation that reform intended to encourage.

Options: Protect opportunities to learn and support state innovation.

—If Congress retains authority to establish national welfare policy, it can encourage experimentation through waivers that include requirements for evaluations.

—If states are given greater control over policy and the need for waivers eliminated, legislation should make clear provision for evaluation of the intended and unintended effects of reforms. HHS should be required to establish evaluation criteria and standards.

—If increased state flexibility is to yield better knowledge about policies and how they work, legislation should reduce the risk to states attempting innovation. This could be done, as suggested in chapter 2, by creating a special fund to underwrite policy experiments and by waiving fiscal sanctions against states that receive grants to experiment with innovative programs or practices.

Toward an Enhanced State Role

Current legislative measures that transfer more responsibility for welfare to the states hinge on the hope that expanding the states' role will pay off in greater efficiency and effectiveness in addressing poverty. However, it will take more than a transfer of responsibilities for states to meet the new challenges they face. States will need support for efforts to build effective programs and to learn from each other's experience. Congress can contribute to making state-based welfare reform more effective by striking a careful balance between flexibility and accountability in crafting reform legislation. It can also contribute by demonstrating its commitment to building state capacity, making certain that states have resources adequate to their responsibilities.

Whether states can develop the capacity to successfully meet enlarged responsibilities for welfare is unknown. Regardless of the precise shape welfare reform takes, state capacity to translate policy goals into effective action will be vital to its future.

5. The Politics of Welfare Reform

R. Kent Weaver

Welfare reform has been on a political roller coaster since Bill Clinton promised in his 1992 presidential campaign to "end welfare as we know it." In its first two years in office, the Clinton administration confronted internal divisions on specific welfare issues, struggled to come up with a financing package to pay for its new welfare initiatives, and repeatedly put welfare reform on the "back burner" to avoid interfering with its health reform initiative.[114]

The new Republican majority in the 104th Congress has also struggled over welfare reform. House Republicans managed to pass a welfare reform plan as one of the last elements of the Contract with America. While the bill won final passage in the House by a wide margin, the earlier vote on the rule to consider the bill came very close to defeat, winning by a narrow 217-211 margin, with 15 Republicans defecting.

When welfare reform moved to the Senate, it quickly became bogged down in disputes over fund distributions, conservative mandates, and other issues. Senate Finance Committee chairman Bob Packwood was able to push the bill quickly through his committee, but floor consideration of the bill was delayed while Majority Leader Robert Dole tried to negotiate a package of changes that would prove acceptable both to conservatives backing a rival bill sponsored by senators Gramm and Faircloth and to moderate Republicans and Democrats. Dole brought his revised bill to the Senate floor in early August but was forced to pull it off the floor after two days (and no votes on amendments or substitutes) when it became clear that he did not have the votes to pass it.

A Dismal History

That initiatives attempting comprehensive welfare reform might run into obstacles should not be a surprise. The history of such initiatives over the past quarter century is largely a history of failure. President Nixon's Family Assistance Plan passed the House but was blocked in the Senate by an odd coalition of conservatives who felt that its income guarantees were unduly generous and liberals who felt that they were too stingy.[115] President Carter's Program for Better Jobs and Incomes (PBJI) proposal also failed to win approval from Congress.[116] One analyst wrote of the Nixon and Carter experiences that "so many factors contributed to the collapse of welfare reform . . . that who or what to blame is almost a matter of whim."[117]

President Reagan managed to push through important changes in the AFDC program as part of the Omnibus Reconciliation Act of 1981, but only one of these changes — limiting most earnings disregards for program recipients to the first four months of earnings — was really a fundamental change in the program.[118] Moreover, 1981 was the high-water mark of the Reagan administration's efforts to transform welfare. President Reagan's "New Federalism" proposal of 1982, which would have resulted in a federal takeover of Medicaid in exchange for giving AFDC and Food Stamps to the states, was never even introduced in Congress.

Politically, the most successful welfare reform initiative in this period was the Family Support Act (FSA) of 1988, which passed the Senate by a vote of 93-3, after a much more contentious battle in the House. The FSA compromise built on a very widely shared perception that the welfare-to-work experiments of the early 1980s showed great promise in improving the earnings of AFDC families.[119] But the FSA was also the most incremental of the major welfare reform initiatives. The Act made a strong rhetorical commitment to improving education, training, transitions to work and child support enforcement, and required the states to meet work participation requirements. But it provided very little in the way of new funding to pay for those commitments.

Old Traps, New Twists

The generally dismal history of efforts at comprehensive welfare reform over the past quarter century is no accident. Such initiatives must maneuver around or through six political traps, outlined below, that affect the design and adoption of welfare reform initiatives. These traps have contributed mightily to the repeated failure or watering down of past initiatives to reform AFDC. The distinctive nature of these traps means that it is almost impossible for policymakers to get something that they see as desirable without also getting something undesirable as a direct consequence.

All of these traps loom large in the current round of welfare reform, often with new and even more perilous twists. Inability to maneuver around or through these traps helped to delay and ultimately sink the Clinton administration's welfare reform initiative in the 103d Congress (1993-94). The contours of these traps have shifted somewhat with the Republican takeover of both houses of Congress in the 1994 election: the nature of the proposals, the coalition of support that must be built and the institutional obstacles to enacting legislation are different. But the basic nature of the traps remains very much the same, and they are proving almost as vexing for the new congressional majority as they did for the Clinton administration and its congressional allies. Passing comprehensive welfare reform legislation in the 104th Congress and reaching an agreement with the president will require extraordinary skill in maneuvering around these traps — and there are not very many strategic options for doing so.

The Dual-Clientele Trap

Perhaps the central political problem for welfare reform initiatives is the dual-clientele trap: policymakers can not take the politically popular step of helping poor children without the politically unpopular step of helping their parents; they can not take the politically popular step of increasing disincentives for out-of-wedlock childbearing without also risking the politically unpopular result that poor children will be made worse off. The fact that the AFDC caseload, like the poverty population generally, is made up heavily of racial and ethnic minorities, has made this debate even more contentious and inflammatory.

Recent welfare reform debates have continually featured a clash between concerns about ensuring the welfare of children against concerns about the behavior (and how to alter it) of parents and prospective parents. The shape of the dual clientele trap has been dramatically altered in this round of welfare reform by the increasing prominence of critiques made by conservative critics of the welfare system like Charles Murray, who argues that "illegitimacy is the single most important social problem of our time — more important than crime, drugs, poverty, illiteracy or homelessness because it drives everything else." As these critiques have been more widely accepted, solutions to the problem of welfare dependency that were once at the margins of the welfare debate became serious legislative proposals. In his 1984 book *Losing Ground*, Murray had proposed ending AFDC and other public assistance programs merely as a "thought experiment." But by 1993, Murray was proposing that single mothers be made ineligible for AFDC, food stamps, and public housing, in order to weaken incentives for, and strengthen social stigma (and parental pressure) against, out-of-wedlock childbirth. For women and girls who continued to have children outside of marriage and were unable to support them, Murray proposed steps to ease adoption, and as a last resort, that governments "spend lavishly on orphanages . . . to provide a warm, nurturing environment" for those children.[120] Conservative critics claimed the moral high ground by arguing that their proposal was actually more beneficial to children than the status quo. Former Secretary of Education Bill Bennett, for example, argued that cutting off welfare and increasing use of foster care and orphanages for children taken from their mothers will actually lead to a lower "body count" of neglected and abused children than the current system.[121]

Although the Clinton administration did not adopt most of the new conservative analysis and rhetoric, its talk of "ending welfare as we know it" implicitly reinforced the wholesale condemnation of AFDC — and the notion that nothing could be worse than the status quo — in the conservative critique. The conservative and Clinton critiques of welfare together had complex implications for the dual clientele trap. On the one hand, they probably weakened the traditional dual clientele trap by softening public and policymaker perceptions that radical changes in AFDC policy necessarily meant making children worse off. At the same time, however, the increasing commitment of many conservatives to proposals such as teen mother exclusions, while liberals continued to reject them, may actually strengthen the dual clientele trap by increasing the policy distance that must be bridged in any compromise: it is easiest to reform welfare, as the 1988 experience showed, when there is widespread agreement on the nature of the problem and the course of reform, when the nature of reform proposals is incremental, and when participants do not take intransigent positions.

The most concrete manifestation of the dual clientele trap in the current round of welfare reform has been debate over conservative proposals to decrease out-of-wedlock births through teen mother exclusions and family caps, and to increase incentives for welfare recipients to find employment by imposing hard time limits on receipt of benefits. How to deal with such proposals created serious problems for the Clinton administration in developing its welfare reform package in 1993-94. Conservatives and "New Democrats" within the Clinton administration pushed for limitations on both cash benefits and subsidized job slots to send a firm message to welfare recipients — and because they felt it was politically necessary to redeem the president's pledge to "end welfare as we know it."[122] Liberals in Congress, upon whom the administration would depend to pass its welfare package, opposed both kinds of time limits — especially leaving recipients without either cash benefits or a job guarantee.[123] Inability to reach a consensus on these issues contributed to the delay in unveiling the administration's welfare reform package until it had been in office almost a year and a half.[124] The Clinton administration ultimately rejected the notion of hard time limits.

The dual clientele trap has also dogged the new Republican majority in Congress in 1995. Changing AFDC and related programs into a block grant offers an opportunity to radically transform the nature of the debate away from concerns about protecting children and toward concerns with meddling by Washington and making government more responsive by giving increased responsibility to the states. If critics charge that Washington is abandoning poor children, defenders of block grants can ask in response why critics think that state governors would be any less willing to defend children than politicians in far-off Washington.

It has not been possible for Republicans to avoid charges of abandoning children entirely by refocusing the debate, however. An early signal that Republicans faced a continuing problem was the debate over orphanages and foster care, as suggested by Murray and Bennett. The original version of the Personal Responsibility Act included in the Contract with America required states to exclude mothers under age 18 from cash benefits (states had the option of excluding mothers up through age 20). States were to be given grants equal to the amount that federal expenditures were reduced by exclusion of those families. Among the purposes for which states could use these funds were "to establish and operate orphanages" and "to establish and operate closely supervised residential homes for unwed mothers."

On the surface, the proposal seemed to be a political plus. It inoculated the Republicans against charges that they were balancing the budget by hurting poor children, and it appeared to offer a solution to the Dual Clientele Trap as well: if (politically popular) poor children were physically separated from (politically unpopular) welfare mothers, the latter could be cut off and the former helped. For several weeks at the end of 1994 and beginning of 1995, the question of orphanages dominated the welfare debate.[125] Experts and pundits debated the efficacy, limitations, and costs of orphanages, as well as when children would be better off living in group situations rather than with their parent or parents.

The orphanage appeal did not play well with the public, however, and Republicans quickly began to back away from a focus on orphanages, arguing that group homes where mothers and children would live together would be a preferred option in most cases.[126] Rising awareness of the high cost of residential facilities for children also dampened their enthusiasm. By mid-January, House Republicans were maneuvering in a House Ways and Means committee hearing to force the Clinton administration's Secretary of Health and Human Services, Donna Shalala, to admit that some children could end up in orphanages under the Clinton administration's welfare proposals, too, if their parents refused to work.[127] By late January, the orphanage issue had largely played itself out. Republicans, including Speaker Gingrich, were heeding the advice of pollster Frank Luntz to avoid mentioning orphanages.[128] With no fresh defenses from the Republicans to serve as a foil, Democrats moved on to other themes in bashing Republican "cruelty." By the time the House Ways and Means Committee began marking up welfare reform legislation in February, orphanages were essentially a dead issue.

While the orphanage issue ultimately proved to be a sideshow in the 1995 welfare reform debate, it did show that the dual clientele debate posed dangers for Republicans as well as Democrats. This became clearer in the evolution of the debate over conservative mandates. While many Republicans, especially young conservatives, backed strong measures intended to reduce illegitimacy, many moderates were more reluctant. Negotiation of the welfare provisions of the Contract with America by a task force made up of both moderate and conservative members was a bitterly divisive process, ultimately resolved through the intervention by then-chair of the House Republican Conference (now Majority Leader) Dick Armey on the side of the conservatives. But divisions between the two camps were still strong enough that after the November 1994 election, Representative Clay Shaw of Florida, the incoming chair of the House Ways and Means Committee's Subcommittee on Human Resources that would have initial jurisdiction over the legislation, threatened to break Republican ranks by not using the Contract provisions as the basis for subcommittee debate on welfare reform — a threat that he quickly backed away from.[129] The notion that Republican bills were "tough on kids" became a consistent theme of Clinton administration attacks throughout the spring and summer of 1995.[130]

The Perverse Incentives Trap

The perverse incentives trap flows from what David Ellwood has called welfare's "helping conundrums." Giving cash to unmarried mothers lowers their incentives to marry or forgo childbearing. Providing them with Medicaid health insurance or child care makes it harder for them to leave AFDC and accept low-paying private-sector jobs that offer no such benefits: if they do, they may suffer real income declines. Providing welfare benefits without reciprocal obligations, most notably the obligation to work, may keep recipients from developing responsibility necessary for success as workers and citizens.

Perverse incentives also feed on themselves: efforts to eliminate or reduce one set can lead to a new set. For example, providing temporary transitional access to Medicaid or child care benefits to families who leave welfare helps them make the transition — but it also encourages people who lose their jobs to go on welfare to take advantage of these benefits before returning to work. No plausible reform of the existing system can avoid creating some new perverse incentives or worsening some existing ones.

The political trap posed by perverse incentives is this: if policymakers ignore those incentives in their reform proposals, public confidence is likely to falter when critics of reform point them out — as they surely will. But coming to grips with those consequences may require spending more, making reform harder to pass as scarce resources are diverted from core reform initiatives.

The Clinton administration encountered the perverse incentives trap in several ways as it tried to develop its welfare reform initiative. First, it relied on health care reform to extend health insurance to the working poor, thus easing the way for AFDC recipients to leave welfare for low-paying jobs. This meant that the projected costs and caseload estimates for welfare reform would be lower (and thus easier to sell politically and to get through the budget scorekeeping process) after comprehensive health care reform passed Congress than before. But the administration could reap these advantages only by delaying welfare reform until after health care reform passed — which it never did.[131]

The Clinton administration also confronted serious concerns that its proposal might lure more people onto the welfare rolls by offering training and child care assistance to recipients.[132] Early drafts of the Clinton plan proposed substantial spending on child care for the working poor to lessen AFDC's attractions for this group. Ultimately, the child care provisions of the bill had to be reduced to meet the limited financing available for the Clinton plan.

The Republican battles over perverse incentives have been different, both because of the way that Republican welfare plans are structured (focusing on disincentives to get on and stay on welfare and work requirements rather than the provision of services) and because the issues that divide Republicans are different. The perverse incentive that concerns many conservative Republicans relates to abortion. Both family caps and teen mother exclusions are expected to increase the number of abortions, and pro-life groups split over the very tough family cap mandates in the House-passed bill.

The Money Trap

The money trap in AFDC politics is simple: any reform likely to improve the prospects for poor children is likely to mean spending more money than the public thinks is necessary or Congress wants to spend. Most people already think that too many people receive AFDC and that too much money is spent on it (see chapter 6 of this volume). But few reform proposals would save money immediately. Instead, they generally require at least short-term spending increases for education, job training, or other services. But to increase spending, government must raise taxes, increase the deficit, or cut other programs — all anathema to legislators. Moreover, current budget rules largely foreclose the option of funding welfare reform by increasing the deficit. So even when Congress adopts welfare reform initiatives, they are underfunded — and therefore hobbled from the start in achieving their goals. The JOBS program of the Family Support Act of 1988, for example, was supposed to have a dramatic impact on the AFDC clientele, while increasing spending only $3 billion over five years for education, training, and employment.

A new wrinkle exacerbating the money trap in this round of welfare reform is the impact of the Budget Enforcement Act (BEA) of 1990. Under the BEA, any legislated changes that increase spending entitlement programs like Social Security, Aid to Families with Dependent Children, Food Stamps, Medicare and most veterans benefits need to be offset by cuts in that program or other entitlements, or by raising additional revenue.[133]

The Budget Enforcement Act procedures complicated the Clinton administration's attempt to formulate a welfare reform package containing new spending on jobs, training, and child care by intensifying the zero-sum nature of budgeting. The administration was reluctant to propose tax increases, and congressional Republicans and conservative Democrats were vehemently opposed to them. No constituencies volunteered to have their taxes increased or benefits cut.[134] Thus cuts in other entitlement programs became the most likely source of funds for welfare reform. But which programs to cut? Social Security? Programs for disabled veterans? Medicare? It did not take a lot of imagination for the Clinton administration's welfare policymakers to imagine the headlines — and the uproar from affected groups — if they appeared to be taking resources from one of these constituencies to give to welfare mothers. The central political challenge for the Clinton administration, then, *was to come up with entitlement programs to cut that are less popular than AFDC.* The problem is that there are not very many entitlements that fit that description. A number of funding proposals, including cutbacks in veterans' benefits and taxation of other means-tested programs, failed to survive the trial balloon stage. Ultimately, the administration relied heavily on benefit cuts to unpopular clienteles — immigrants and persons deemed disabled as a result of drug and alcohol abuse — to finance much of their welfare reform proposal. But the administration's welfare reform plan was delayed, and ultimately cut back, because they could not come up with adequate funding.

The Clinton administration could have maneuvered around these budget rules in two ways, but each option has its problems. The first option was to use the administration's initial 1993 budget package to finance welfare reform. The budget package involved significant tax increases: if a welfare reform proposal had been included in that package (as the expansion of the Earned Income Tax Credit was), it would avoid the necessity of being directly pitted against other programs and clienteles for funds. Using this route had a couple of problems, however: the budget package was on a "fast track," with the administration hoping to complete action within the first one hundred days after coming into office. But to "end welfare as we know it" requires extraordinarily detailed legislation; it is a far more complex legislative (and administrative) task than expanding the EITC. And given the controversial nature of AFDC, including welfare reform in the budget package risked bogging down the latter and giving it a less popular political face. Moreover, "deficit hawks" within the administration and Congress were determined to use the budget package to reduce the deficit and wanted to reserve as much as possible of the "enhanced revenue" for that purpose. As a result, welfare reform was not included in the administration's 1993 budget package.[135]

A second way to get around the Budget Enforcement Act's "pay-as-you-go" strictures was to put most of the program expansion — and increased spending — after the five year-window on which "pay-as-you-go" is calculated. As will be discussed further below, the administration did indeed do this with its phase-in provisions for younger mothers. The problem with this approach is that the administration did not appear to be "ending welfare as we know it" within its first term in office. Indeed, the House Republicans' welfare reform bill in the 103d

Congress, unveiled seven months *before* Clinton's, put tougher work requirements in place more quickly (in part because they were willing to be much tougher on restricting benefits to immigrants than the Clinton administration and cap expenditure growth in many means-tested programs), while still cutting overall expenditures.

Republican proposals in the 104th Congress have continued down the path begun by their 1993 proposal. But the money trap has been radically transformed, and exacerbated, by the Republican deficit reduction initiative. It requires massive cuts in means-tested programs, at the same time that work requirements are being steeply increased — and providing work and training costs more than simply sending checks to recipients. If neither work mandates nor deficit reduction are to be sacrificed, the only other option is to ship the problem off to the states as an unfunded mandate. Not surprisingly, this is the option that emerged in the course of congressional debate. Work requirements in the Contract with America were softened to bring Republican governors on board as allies for welfare reform at the beginning of the year. However, they were gradually stiffened again as the legislation moved through the House, in response to criticisms from both Republican conservatives and the Clinton administration that the legislation was "weak on work." Whether the work mandate issue will ultimately lead to an unravelling of the alliance between congressional Republicans and Republican governors remains to be seen.

The Overselling Trap

With AFDC so unpopular, its clientele so politically weak, and the record of derailed reform so long, legislators are reluctant to undertake reform for only modest policy gains. Hence the overselling trap: to get welfare reform on the agenda, much less pass it, advocates of reform generally must promise far more than they can deliver. Overselling has serious costs, however. Not only does it threaten the credibility of specific reform proposals, it also increases public cynicism about any reform. If reform did not produce significant improvements last time, why will it do so this time? Thus politicians grow even more reluctant to wade into the welfare reform swamp, necessitating yet more over-promising — and so the cycle goes.

The overselling trap in the current round of welfare reform began with the president's claims that he would "end welfare as we know it." Having made this commitment, administration policymakers felt that they would be politically hammered by the Republicans if they did not come up with a proposal that could plausibly be portrayed as doing so. Indeed, post-election research by the new administration's pollsters showed that welfare reform ranked third on the list of what the public perceived to be the administration's most important promises.[136] The image conveyed to the public in the Clinton administration's June 1994 reform proposal was that of an income transfer program being transformed into a work program: recipients could receive benefits for only two years before being expected to work.

The reality of the Clinton administration's proposal was quite different, however. Many welfare mothers were not expected to work, either because they are caring for infants or because they are seriously disabled or care for children who are. An even bigger hurdle was money. Providing jobs, even low-paying jobs, takes lots of it — for administration, transportation, and child care. Providing jobs to all AFDC parents could cost over $20 billion a year. Thus the Clinton plan called for a slow phase-in (beginning with younger mothers) and many exemptions. By the year 2000, parents in less than 10 percent of total AFDC cases were projected to be at work in government provided or subsidized jobs.[137] Such a phase-in was both fiscally necessary and administratively prudent, but it does not constitute "ending welfare as we know it" — at least not in the short-term. Republicans immediately denounced the plan as "weak on work."

Republicans have encountered the overselling trap as well. Concessions made to Republican governors easing work participation requirements in early versions of the House bill came under fire by Democrats as "weak on work, "and caused those requirements to be stiffened as legislation moved through the House of Representatives. Whether states will have the administrative capacity and fiscal resources needed to meet the work requirements in current bills remains to be seen.

The Federalism Trap

States currently have great leeway both in the AFDC benefits they pay and in the obligations they impose. States can also apply for waivers to deviate from existing federal standards, and more than two-thirds of all states have had waivers granted to them.

Allowing states flexibility offers a number of potential advantages, from creating more "laboratories of democracy" for policy experimentation to allowing more responsiveness to local preferences (see chapter 2 of this volume). But permitting state discretion also poses what can be called the federalism trap: federal policymakers cannot give states the discretion to do things they would like without also running the risk that states will also do things that they do not like.

Liberals have been particularly concerned that state flexibility may subject individuals to extremely unequal treatment based on where they live, or start a "race to the bottom," as states scale back benefits and impose ever more onerous obligations to avoid becoming welfare magnets. The federalism trap has been especially difficult for the Clinton administration because of the president's record as a former governor who professes great faith in the states. Thus the administration included family caps as a state option in its welfare plan despite skepticism from its own officials that doing so would make a noticeable dent in welfare caseloads. In addition, it has sent signals that it will approve virtually any state waiver request, regardless of how it may conflict with the administration's policy preferences.

Social conservatives have had a different set of fears: unless mandates are imposed on the states, they may fail to undertake on their own the kinds of initiatives against out-of-wedlock births that conservatives favor. In 1995 many social conservatives have argued that it is irresponsible to give states money without mandating disincentives such as family caps and a ban on benefits to teen mothers.[138] In these conflicts, social conservatives have been pitted against Republican governors, who favor block grants with as few strings attached as possible. As Governor John Engler of Michigan has put it, "Conservative micromanagement is just as bad as liberal micromanagement."[139] This conflict has played out throughout the development of Republican welfare reform legislation this year. After the 1994 election, a group of Republican governors realized that budget cuts were inevitable in the new Congress. They negotiated a revised welfare reform package with Republican leaders in Congress that gave them more flexibility, and weaker mandates, than the welfare reform proposals in the Contract with America. Many of these gains were in turn eroded as the bill moved through the House of Representatives, the social conservatives' institutional stronghold. As the bill moved to the Senate, the governors had another bargaining opportunity to recoup those gains. They were largely successful in doing so in the bills developed first by the Senate Finance Committee and later by Senator Dole. But they were stalemated when Senator Dole was unable to steer his bill through to passage.

The Fragile Coalition Trap

Once welfare reform proposals reach Congress, all of the problems created by the traps outlined above are manifested in what can be called the fragile coalitions trap: no legislative majority can be built for reform without incorporating legislators who disagree with some elements of the package, and are likely to defect if separate votes are held on those individual elements. Elements of the package that increase spending and those that create or redress perverse incentives are especially vulnerable to being peeled off. This, of course, may alienate other elements of the coalitions whose support is contingent on maintaining those features of the reform package. The risk of a collapsing coalition can be minimized if sponsors of welfare reform can control the agenda to reject consideration of threatening amendments, but they usually cannot, especially in the Senate.

Clinton's coalition was particularly prone to defections and ultimate collapse. Liberals Democrats opposed provisions they feared would deprive many families of cash benefits. Conservative Democrats did not like its slow phase-in of work requirements. The Hispanic Caucus objected to the cutbacks to immigrant benefits in its financing provisions. Public sector unions worried that a large public jobs program would displace their workers, while conservatives feared that it could turn into another CETA public service employment program.

If the Clinton administration had come out with a welfare reform plan early in its first two years, it might have been able to forge a compromise on many of these issues and get a welfare reform bill through Congress, especially if they were willing to draw some elements from H.R. 3500, House Republicans' welfare reform bill in the 103d Congress. But the administration's repeated delays in getting a package to Congress, and unclear signals about how quickly it wanted action once the package was released (caused in part by a desire to keep the decks clear for health care reform) meant that there were only a few months left between the June 1994 unveiling of the package and the November election.

By the late summer of 1994, however, congressional Republicans were anticipating substantial gains in the fall election, so they had no incentive to facilitate quick passage of welfare reform: delaying consideration of welfare until the new Congress would increase the prospects of getting a welfare reform package closer to the median preferences of Republican legislators, would deny the president a legislative victory and the credit that would therefore accrue to him, and would allow Republican candidates to continue to use the welfare issue that was working very well for them in the election campaign.[140] While the House Ways and Means Committee held hearings on the Clinton proposal in the summer of 1994, they never proceeded to mark up the bill, let alone report it to the full chamber.

Republicans have also confronted the fragile coalition trap in building support for welfare reform legislation in the current Congress. The basic challenge facing Republican congressional leaders has been to find compromises that will hold together Republican moderates and conservatives, especially on the "conservative mandate" issues, while preserving an alliance with the leading Republican governors and neutralizing the intergovernmental lobby. At the same time, they have to prevent defections by their own special constituency oriented members, notably those with a strong right-to-life orientation.

That they succeeded in doing so in the House of Representatives is a tribute to an extraordinarily effective Republican leadership. But it also reflects strong individual and collective incentives for the coalition partners to hold together and to try to pass a compromise that they all could live with and an astute use of the House Rules Committee to prevent challenges likely to sink the bill.

The most obvious collective incentive for Republican legislators was the desire to show Republican unity — and in particular to demonstrate that the Republicans could govern effectively and end gridlock. In addition, there was a desire to avoid losing the welfare issue back to the Democrats. President Clinton had used the issue of welfare reform effectively in the 1992 election, but the House Republicans, with their very aggressive stance, had regained the initiative, and public confidence (see figure 6-2 in chapter 6) in 1994. The Republicans had no desire to cede it back. And while there were deep substantive divisions among House Republicans on some elements of the Personal Responsibility Act, virtually none of them wanted a stalemate to ensue, which would likely result in the policy status quo remaining in place. The timing of House consideration of welfare reform was also a help: because it came at the end of the "One Hundred Days," there was enormous pressure on Republican members to vote for the bill to "complete the Contract"; there was, moreover, enormous exhaustion on the part of House GOP members — both conditions that are likely to advantage the leadership. Finally, the Republican leadership benefitted from the fact that most Republican members did not have a strong constituency interest in resisting the cutbacks to means-tested programs contained in the Personal Responsibility Act. With a few exceptions (for example, Cuban American representatives from Florida, whose constituents would be disproportionately affected by the immigrant provisions of the Act), most House Republican members did not face strong constituent resistance to the legislation.

There were also strong incentives for each of the partners in the House Republican coalition to go along with the welfare reform package negotiated in the House. GOP conservatives, who gained most of what they wanted in the House bill, had perhaps the greatest incentive to agree. The activist Republican governors, who had lost ground as the bill moved through the House, were more likely to advance their interests by retaining what they could in the House bill by being supportive, and recognizing that they would have another opportunity to reshape the bill when it went to the Senate. GOP moderates who had reservations about the bill could also be comforted by the idea that this was not the final word on welfare reform. The Senate was widely expected to moderate whatever the House did on welfare, so it made little strategic sense to oppose the bill at this point.[141]

The Republican leadership was also extremely effective in using the Rules Committee in the House to reward those interests who cooperated and keep divisive issues off the agenda. For example, representatives allied with right-to-life groups and Roman Catholic bishops were given an opportunity to present an amendment, with leadership support, that allowed states to use federal funds to give vouchers to teen mothers and those affected by a family cap who would no longer be eligible for federal funding for cash benefits. Moderate Republican leader Nancy Johnson was allowed to offer an amendment that increased funding for child care for mothers subject to the work requirement. But amendments that threatened to split the Republican coalition were not allowed.

House Republicans did not succeed in winning many Democrats over to their bill, however. Democrats were sharply divided within themselves, and the more liberal of two Democratic substitute bills that the Rules Committee allowed to come to a vote was overwhelmingly defeated. But Democrats united around a conservative Democratic alternative (sponsored by a soon-to-be Republican, Nathan Deal of Georgia) and stayed united in opposing House final passage of the Republican bill.[142] Thus the House debate contained both good news and bad news for Republicans. On the good news front, President Clinton had backed the Deal bill despite the fact that it contained hard time limits, something the administration had ultimately backed down from doing in its own welfare package the previous June. Thus the president had been nudged an important step to the right. But on the negative side, the unity of the Democrats in the House suggested that it would probably be hard to gain Democratic support for a Republican bill in the Senate where, given that body's non-majoritarian procedures, help from some members of the minority party would be needed.

The narrow margin of Republican control in the Senate and the opportunities for minority obstruction are by themselves substantial obstacles to passage of welfare reform legislation. In 1995 they have been complicated further by presidential politics. Senate Majority Leader Robert Dole, the leading Republican contender, faced dual, and somewhat conflicting, pressures. As the only presidential contender in a congressional leadership position, Dole needed to show that he was an effective leader in getting legislation passed — never an easy task in the fractious and individualistic Senate. Dole's personal policy preferences also suggested attempting a bipartisan approach to welfare: in January, he criticized the evolving House Republican bill on welfare reform — and in particular its ban on cash benefits to young mothers — as overly radical.[143] But Dole faced competition in the Republican primaries from competitors placing themselves to his right — notably Senator Phil Gramm — and he was under pressure to move in that direction to appeal to conservative activists who tend to vote disproportionately in Republican primaries.[144] Senator Gramm and his allies backed a rival bill modeled after the House-passed measure and had little incentive at this point to back down and acquiesce in a Dole bill that did not fit their policy preferences and would give a political boost to Dole. Republican moderates resisted moving further to the right, and Senate Democrats united behind a bill sponsored by Minority Leader Tom Daschle that preserved entitlement status for family assistance payments. The conflict was further complicated by a funding formula fight between Sunbelt senators who feared that their rapidly growing states would lose out under existing funding allotments and northern senators who did not want to give up funding to their states.[145] While Dole was able to temporarily patch up the formula fight by promising more money for high-growth states, he could not resolve the mandates issues. With limited leverage to compel the other camps to follow his lead, little prospect that adjusting his own position would lead to a majority (even if a filibuster by conservatives could be avoided), and without the agenda control afforded by the House rules process, Dole's effort to push welfare reform through before the August recess collapsed before voting on any amendments began.

Avoiding the Traps

While the contours of the traps that have bedeviled past comprehensive welfare reform initiatives have been altered, and partially obscured, by the thrust of the current Republican initiative, they are still very much in existence, and still very formidable. Some traps that Republican leaders have thus far largely succeeded in papering over could easily reemerge at any time to confound this round of welfare reform. These traps are not insurmountable, however. Republican leaders in Congress have several important things working in their favor going into the welfare reform battle this fall.

Weak Public and Interest Group Opposition

As noted in chapter 6 of this volume, the American public has very negative attitudes toward the current welfare system, but it is ambivalent about many of the proposed solutions. However, what are arguably the most important provisions of this round of welfare reform for the long-term — conversion of AFDC and related programs into a largely fixed-sum block grant — have very little resonance with the public. While the prospects are high that conversion to a block grant would lead to a major erosion of expenditures on family support payments over time, this is a process that is little understood by the public and hard to explain. To the extent that a potential debate about the welfare of children is transformed into a debate about federalism, strong opposition in the public and the press is unlikely to emerge. The most likely losers from reform are the states, but so long as state leaders believe that cuts are inevitable, and the intergovernmental lobby is effectively neutralized, this will not be an insurmountable obstacle to Republican welfare reform initiatives.

Meeting Budget Targets

Another important impetus for the Republicans to hang together and pass welfare reform this year is that they need the money to meet the extremely ambitious deficit reduction targets they have set. The Clinton administration estimates that the House-passed bill will produce almost $70 billion in expenditure reductions over five years, while S. 1120, the bill introduced by Senator Dole, will produce savings of almost $50 billion.[146] It is very doubtful that they can reach their budget targets without a major contribution from welfare expenditure reductions.

Reconciliation

An important procedural advantage the Republican majority in Congress has to push welfare reform through Congress is the availability of the budget reconciliation process. Congress is expected to consider a reconciliation bill later this fall to enact changes in mandatory spending programs needed to meet their budgetary targets.

Rolling welfare reform into a reconciliation bill offers several benefits for the Republicans in avoiding the fragile coalitions trap. One set of benefits concerns the incentives reconciliation creates for Republican unity. First, folding a vote on welfare reform into an omnibus bill covering dozens or hundreds of programs makes the elements of the welfare reform bill with which individual legislators disagree relatively less visible and salient than they would be if welfare were being considered separately. Second, since seriousness about deficit reduction is a major part of congressional Republicans' political message, there is a strong incentive for Republican legislators to make sure that the reconciliation package passes. (Deep cuts in Medicare and Medicaid will strain Republican unity on deficit reduction, however). Third, a reconciliation bill is likely to be considered very quickly after it is agreed upon by Republican leaders in Congress; opponents will have very little time to organize. For all three of these reasons, Republican party unity on the reconciliation bill is likely to be very high; whatever qualms Republican legislators might have about individual provisions of the welfare bill, they are likely to hold their noses and vote yes.

Reconciliation also has even more important advantages for getting welfare reform past Democratic opposition. The most critical is the limitation of debate on reconciliation bills to twenty hours in the Senate. A determined minority cannot use a filibuster or threat of a filibuster to block passage of welfare reform if it is included in reconciliation.

Weak Bargaining Position of the President

Another advantage the Republicans have in getting a welfare reform bill through in 1995 is the relatively weak bargaining position of the president. President Clinton, having pledged to "end welfare as we know it," will be hard pressed to veto any welfare reform proposal (whether as a separate piece of legislation or as part of reconciliation) that does just that by converting it into from an entitlement into a block grant and imposing stiff work requirements. Indeed, the administration has resisted efforts to commit the president to a bottom line of what the president would not accept — in part because of fears that the Republicans would come right up to that point. There is, however, a risk that some Republicans may push the party to overplay their hand for political gain, risking passage of welfare reform for the electoral opportunity to present the president as a hypocrite who was not really committed to welfare reform.[147]

Prospects for Reform

There are two primary routes that welfare reform can take in the remainder of the 104th Congress. The first is a partisan-based strategy, in which the Republican majority unites around a budget reconciliation bill and uses the debate-limiting nature of the reconciliation process to bring home wayward Republican troops and avoid stalling tactics by coalitions of minorities opposed to one or more provisions of their party's plans. This essentially is a variation on the strategy pursued by President Reagan in 1981. While this route is complicated in 1995 by the fact that President Clinton is from a different party, the weak bargaining power of the president may allow this strategy to succeed.

The other path is to seek middle ground — the path eventually pursued successfully in 1988 round of welfare reform. This path would involve seeking a compromise with President Clinton and a number of Democrats on some key issues — notably the conservative mandates on family caps and teen mother exclusions — and cooperation on many issues where the distances are less (for example, work requirements, child support enforcement, and even hard time limits). Perhaps most important, Republicans could almost certainly win conversion of AFDC into a block grant — a change that chapter 2 of this volume argues is by itself likely to lead to a dramatic change in the resources available to aid poor families over time.

The desire of conservative Republicans to pursue the first path and change the welfare system as much as they can during the first session of the 104th Congress is understandable. Political coalitions favoring radical change tend to be unstable, and the electoral future of that coalition is by no means assured. But past rounds of welfare reform suggest that a partisan-based strategy, while it can produce more dramatic change, has high risks. More often than not, comprehensive initiatives designed to transform the nature of the welfare system have ended in stalemate, the perpetuation of the status quo, and heightened reluctance by politicians to take up in the near future an issue that appears to offer few political or policy rewards. If conservative Republicans hold out for a whole loaf, they risk repeating the historical role played by liberals who helped kill President Nixon's Family Assistance Plan, hoping that they could get a better deal at a later historical moment. Instead, history passed them by, and a rare opportunity (although far from a certainty) to transform the American welfare state was missed.

The legislative process in the United States is extraordinarily fragmented. It digests and sustains small legislative steps far more easily than large ones. A window of opportunity for radical transformation of the welfare system — for better or for ill — seems to be at hand. But the history of welfare reform suggests that because of the omnipresent traps confounding comprehensive welfare reform, what seemed to be windows at the time may appear in retrospect to have been mirages all along. Even when the windows of opportunity are real, they can disappear quickly, never appearing in the same form again.

The history of welfare reform suggests another lesson as well. Even if Congress does enact a dramatic welfare reform this year, it will not be the end of the story. No initiative currently foreseeable can resolve the underlying social problems that programs to aid poor families try to address. Welfare reform will be back on the agenda, and so will the traps that make its politics so painful and its results seem so meager.

6. Public Opinion on Welfare Reform: A Mandate for What?

R. Kent Weaver, Robert Y. Shapiro and Lawrence R. Jacobs[*]

The debate over welfare, a generic and ambiguous label for public assistance programs in the United States that is most commonly applied to the Aid to Families with Dependent Children (AFDC) program, has changed dramatically since Bill Clinton pledged in his 1992 campaign for the presidency to "end welfare as we know it" and to move people from income assistance to work. In the abstract, a bipartisan consensus has long favored work instead of cash welfare payments and has favored significant welfare reform.[148] The current controversy is over how to reform welfare. Republicans are pushing for reforms that will turn over increased responsibility to the states, increase disincentives to out-of-wedlock births, and reduce federal expenditures. The Clinton administration's proposal stressed the need to provide additional child care and job guarantees while protecting poor children.

Both the Clinton administration and Republicans have invested heavily in trying to influence how the public sees the welfare issue and trying to associate the other party with unpopular positions.[149] Republicans charge that the existing system is full of perverse incentives for parents — most notably the incentive to have children out of wedlock at government expense — and argue that "what is really cruel is the current incentive that pulls young women into the system and holds them forever in this cruel trap."[150] Democrats and childrens' advocacy groups argue that Republicans should not finance tax breaks to the wealthy by cutting benefits and services to poor children.[151] Both sides have charged the other with being "weak on work." And both sides perceive the stakes to be very high: the side that is able to convince the public that its vision of welfare and proposed solutions are the most appropriate ones will have an advantage in winning enactment of its proposals, and perhaps also in future electoral contests.

[*]The authors' research, which is part of a larger collaborative project on the Clinton administration and social policy, has been supported by the Russell Sage Foundation. They thank Theo Noell, Greg Shaw, Matt Stevens, and Cindy Terrels for their assistance, as well as Gilbert Y. Steiner for comments, and Jennifer Baggette and Lois Timms-Ferrara for help with data collection. The responsibility for analysis and interpretation is the authors.

How successful have these efforts to shape public opinion been? This chapter examines the recent evolution of public opinion toward the current welfare system, welfare recipients, and leading proposals for welfare reform.[152] We seek to shed light on three questions in the welfare debate. To what extent is public opinion on welfare shifting?[153] To what extent is welfare reform being driven by, or at least supported by, changing public opinion? To what extent has public opinion coalesced around a specific set of policy proposals or is likely to coalesce in the future?

Although important changes in public opinion have occurred recently, the most fundamental characteristic of American attitudes toward means-tested programs, especially Aid to Families with Dependent Children, is a deep and durable ambivalence that stems from the dual clientele of the program: poor children and their parents (usually single mothers).[154] The public feels great sympathy toward and wants to protect poor children. But it also resents those parents whom it perceives to be acting irresponsibly or cheating the system. The public also fears that AFDC saps initiative and offers perverse incentives. This deep ambivalence is often not captured by simplistic survey questions that force respondents to choose between simple responses with no nuances. The overview of public opinion presented here therefore traces changes in opinion over time and shows how differences in wording affect public responses. This deep ambivalence also means that although Republican and Democratic leaders can move the welfare debate in one direction or another, it is unlikely that either conservatives or liberals can win the debate over the proper direction for welfare reform and use it as a basis for partisan realignment.

What Is Welfare?

A basic problem in analyzing public opinion toward welfare and welfare reform is that it may not be clear what the public means by the terms when responding to questions, since many surveys often do not identify specific programs. Does the public associate welfare just with AFDC or more broadly with other means-tested programs from Food Stamps to Head Start to Medicaid and Supplemental Security Income? A January 1995 survey for the Kaiser Family Foundation suggests that *when prompted by the names of specific programs*, the public identifies a very broad array of means-tested programs as welfare, and will exclude contributory social insurance programs (Social Security and Medicare) from that definition. People also overestimate the share of the federal budget that is spent on means-tested programs.[155] It is less clear, however, whether the broad concept of welfare is triggered by general survey questions about welfare that do not include prompts about specific programs.

A second problem in analyzing public opinion on welfare stems from the phenomenon long noted by researchers that public opinion on programs for low-income Americans differs significantly depending on the precise wording of questions — most notably between questions relating to "welfare" and those relating to "programs for poor children." "Welfare" is likely to stimulate responses focusing on parents, and in particular on images of abuse and fraud by welfare recipients.[156] It is also likely to stimulate associations with racial minorities. The term "poor children," however, stimulates images of a sympathetic clientele that is not responsible for its own condition.[157]

Attitudes toward the Current System

Discontent with the current system of public assistance is very strong and widespread, and it has increased in recent years (table 6-1). Other data reveal that only one-sixth of Americans polled at the end of 1993 thought that the welfare system was working very well or fairly well, while 79 percent thought that it was not working very well or not well at all. This put the welfare system at the bottom of six policy sectors rated in the poll — even lower than the criminal justice system.[158]

Table 6-1. Does the Welfare System Work Well?[a]

Percent unless otherwise specified

Polling organization/sponsor	ABC/Washington Post	ABC/Washington Post
Number surveyed	n.a.	1,145
Month of poll	12/85	1/95
Yes	39	25
No	56	72
Don't know, no opinion	5	3

n.a. Not available.

[a]Question: As you may know, the government gives poor people money through welfare and public assistance programs, including food stamps and aid to dependent children. Overall would you say the system of public assistance works well in this country, or not?

See note on table sources at the end of the volume.

The most basic judgment that the public can make about the efficacy of a program is whether it does more harm than good. The welfare system fails this test: in an April 1995 survey 69 percent of the public agreed with the statement that "the welfare system does more harm than good, because it encourages the breakup of the family and discourages work." Only 23 percent believed that "the welfare system does more good than harm, because it provides assistance and training for those who are without jobs and are poor." This ratio does not seem to have been affected significantly by the vociferous debate in the House of Representatives, and in the country, in the first months of 1995.[159] By margins of more than seven to one, the public thinks that the current system causes people to become dependent and stay poor rather than giving them a chance to stand on their own feet.[160] Both questions, it should be noted, focus primarily on the effects of the welfare system on parents rather than the protection of children, and the system is clearly judged a failure on this criterion. Much of the public is concerned that welfare benefits may be too high, that the system encourages long-term dependence, discourages work, and causes women to have more children than they would if they did not go on welfare.[161] Welfare, in short, is perceived as being at odds with the widely shared American belief in individualism and the work ethic.

Most Americans — almost two-thirds in 1995 polls — also think that too much is being spent on welfare (table 6-2). That percentage has increased from about 40 percent of those surveyed to around 65 percent in the past four years. Part of that change is probably due to the increase in AFDC expenditures since the late 1980s: the percentage of the public that believes too much is being spent on welfare generally rises when AFDC expenditures increase. There is also a strong relationship between the party of the incumbent president and public opinion on welfare spending. When Democrats control the presidency, some part of the public apparently assumes that governments must be spending too much on welfare. When Republicans are in control, there is an automatic assumption that government is being too stingy.[162] A similar shift in public opinion against welfare spending occurred in the late 1970s. But the unprecedently high levels of support for the position that too much is being spent on welfare by the end of 1994 suggest that conservative arguments about bloated welfare programs are meeting with some success.

There are, however, significant ambiguities in the data, and wording changes make a major difference in the findings of survey research. The same surveys that show overwhelming rejection of spending on "welfare" show that strong majorities believe too little is being spent on "assistance to the poor," and "government spending on programs for poor children," although support for these positions has also eroded significantly over the past few years (table 6-2). Moreover, when asked in November 1993 whether the "the bigger problem with the welfare system today" is that "it spends too much money" or "it spends money the wrong way," 85 percent of those surveyed argued that it was spending money the wrong way that was the bigger problem, compared to only 4 percent for "spends too much money."[163] But although public support for cutting welfare expenditures to reduce the budget deficit has increased greatly since the late 1980s, public willingness to spend more for job training and public service jobs remains high and stable (tables 6-3 and 6-4).

Table 6-2. Public Opinion on Welfare Spending

Percent

Month/year	Welfare spending				Assistance to the poor				Spending on poor children			
	Too much	About right	Too little	Too much–too little	Too much	About right	Too little	Too much–too little	Too much	About right	Too little	Too much–too little
4/95	66	18	9	57	...	...	...	...	...	...	...	...
1/95	67	19	10	57	...	...	...	...	...	...	...	...
12/94	64	17	12	52	...	...	...	...	...	...	...	...
12/94	48	36	13	35	...	...	...	...	9	39	47	-38
3/94	60	24	13	47	15	25	57	-42	...	...	...	...
11/93	55	24	14	41	...	...	...	...	6	22	64	-58
3/93	54	25	16	38	12	22	63	-51	...	...	...	...
3/91	38	35	22	16	9	22	65	-56	...	...	...	...
3/90	38	35	22	16	7	24	66	-59	...	...	...	...
3/89	42	30	23	19	9	23	66	-57	...	...	...	...
3/88	42	32	23	19	7	23	68	-61	...	...	...	...
3/87	44	31	21	23	9	23	66	-57	...	...	...	...
3/86	40	34	22	18	9	27	61	-52	...	...	...	...
3/85	45	33	19	26	10	25	63	-53	...	...	...	...
3/84	40	33	24	16	11	24	62	-51	...	...	...	...
3/83	47	28	21	26	...	...	...	...	...	...	...	...
3/82	48	28	20	28	...	...	...	...	...	...	...	...
3/80	57	26	13	44	...	...	...	...	...	...	...	...
3/78	58	25	13	45	...	...	...	...	...	...	...	...
3/77	60	23	12	48	...	...	...	...	...	...	...	...
3/76	60	22	13	47	...	...	...	...	...	...	...	...
3/75	43	29	23	20	...	...	...	...	...	...	...	...
3/74	42	32	22	20	...	...	...	...	...	...	...	...
3/73	51	24	20	31	...	...	...	...	...	...	...	...

See notes on sources and question wording at end of volume.

Table 6-3. Support for Welfare Cuts to Reduce the Deficit

Percent unless otherwise specified

Polling organization/sponsor	ABC/*WP*[a]	ABC/*WP*[a]	ABC/*WP*[b]	YP for *Time*/ CNN[c]
Number surveyed	n.a.	1,145	1,011	800
Month of poll	11/88	1/95	5/95	5/95
Yes/cut	27	54	44	65
No/prevent cuts	66	40	52	29
No opinion	7	6	2	6

[a]"In order for the federal government to cut spending to reduce the budget deficit, would you support or oppose reducing welfare, or public assistance, for poor people?"

[b]"In order to reduce the federal budget deficit, should the government cut spending on . . . welfare, or public assistance for poor people, or not?"

[c]"I'm going to read you a list of programs that some people have suggested be cut to balance the budget by the year 2002. For each, please tell me if it is more important to make significant cuts in that program to balance the budget or whether you think it is more important to prevent that program from being cut . . . Welfare programs."

Table 6-4. Willingness to Pay for Job Training and Public Service Jobs[a]

Percent unless otherwise specified

Polling organization/sponsor	CBS/*New York Times*	CBS/*New York Times*	CBS/*New York Times*
Number surveyed	1,146	1,147	1,089
Month of poll	1/94	12/94	4/95
Willing	61	59	61
Unwilling	34	37	35
Don't know/no answer	5	4	4

[a]"Would you be willing or unwilling to pay more in taxes in order to provide job training and public service jobs for people on welfare so that they can get off welfare?"

The most plausible explanation of different survey results for questions with different wordings is that much of the public is more concerned with getting a welfare system that they think is more consistent with their own beliefs and values[164] (and less ridden with fraud and perverse incentives) than they are with using changes in the welfare system to produce deficit reduction. This argument is supported by polls that have asked respondents what they think are the most important goals that should be pursued in a welfare reform initiative. Moving welfare recipients into the workforce, ending dependence on welfare as a way of life, and giving recipients skills needed to make them self-sufficient consistently end up as top goals; saving money for taxpayers comes in near the bottom (table 6-5).

Table 6-5. Public Opinion on the Most Important Goals of Welfare Reform[a]

Percent unless otherwise specified

Goals	Yankelovich Clancy Shulman for *Time*/CNN	Yankelovich Clancy Shulman for *Time*/CNN	Hart/Teeter[b]	*Los Angeles Times*	NBC/ *Wall Street Journal*[b]
Number surveyed	1,400	1,250	1,020	1,682	505
Month of poll	3/92	5/92	11/93	4/94	3/95
Reduce out-of-wedlock births	...	...	...	17	15
Help move people now on welfare into the workforce	...	...	52	73	45
Make sure poor children get the support they need	...	...	22	...	17
Eliminate fraud and abuse	...	...	28	...	29
Give people skills to make them self-sufficient	90	93	...	...	...
End long-term dependence on welfare as a way of life	...	...	29	...	51
Save taxpayers money, cut costs	5	3	7	6	...
Other (vol.)	...	...	...	1	...
All (vol.)	3	2	...	...	9
Not sure, don't know	3	2	1	3	...

[a]"What should the most important goal of welfare reform be?" Exact wording varies slightly. Where no percentage appears next to a goal, it was not included as an option in that poll.

[b]Up to two responses permitted.

Causes of Poverty and Welfare Dependence

Too often, poll questions trying to ascertain the public's beliefs about why people are poor and become dependent on welfare programs are posed in terms of overly simplistic dichotomies: for example, does receiving welfare result more from poor motivations or from circumstances beyond people's control, or from poor values or bad policies. Given these choices, the public's responses emphasize to individual failings, and the percentage has increased dramatically in the past four years (figure 6-1). Respondents also think that a large number of welfare recipients should not be receiving benefits.[165] However, when surveys offer several possible reasons for receiving welfare, large percentages of the public appear to have fairly sophisticated and complex beliefs about why people are poor or receive welfare, emphasizing both socioeconomic problems such as a shortage of jobs, poor education, and a breakdown in families and individual failings such as poor motivation (table 6-6). Even many of those who believe that large segments of the poor are to blame for their condition also believe that government has a duty to care for those who cannot care for themselves, although that responsibility is not unlimited in duration (table 6-7).[166]

Table 6-6. Perceived Causes of Poverty[a]

	Mean	(10-8)	(7-5)	(4-1)	Not sure
Poor people lacking motivation	6.1	29	52	18	1
Absent parents not paying child support	7.0	49	35	15	1
Increased immigration	6.3	39	35	23	3
A shortage of jobs	6.7	42	39	18	1
The welfare system	6.9	45	38	15	2
The breakdown of families and family values	7.6	60	29	10	1
Poor people receiving inadequate education	6.9	46	36	16	2
Too many jobs being part time or low wage	6.6	42	37	20	1

Source: Telephone poll of 1,020 respondents conducted between November 12-15, 1993 by Peter D. Hart Research Associates.

[a]For each of the following, tell me how big a factor it is in causing poverty, on a scale from 1 to 10. A rating of 1 means the item is *not* a cause at all, a 10 means it is a top cause of poverty, and a 5 is somewhere in the middle. Remember, you may use any number between 1 and 10, depending on how you feel. First, how big a cause of poverty is this on a scale from 1 to 10?

Figure 6-1. Public Opinion on Causes of Poverty, 1982-95: "What Is More Likely to Blame When People Are Poor/ When People Receive Welfare?"

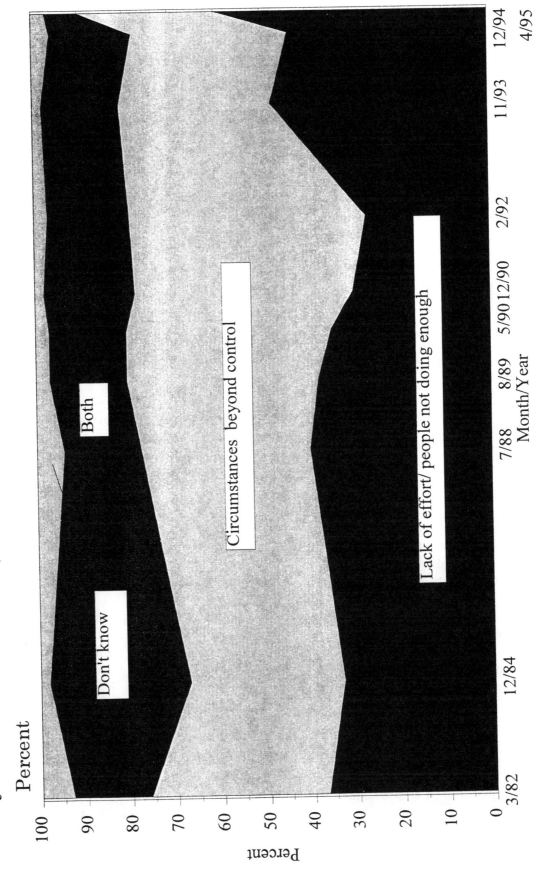

Table 6-7. Public Opinion on Service Approaches to Welfare Reform

Percent in favor of/agreeing with option:

	TMLL for USNWR	Hart/ Teeter	Gallup	KRC for Harvard/ Kaiser	Hart/ Teeter for *WSJ*
Number surveyed	1,000	1,020		1,200	1,504
Month of poll	11/93	11/93	4/94	12/94	4/95
Provide job training	. . .	. . .	94	87	95
Provide child care so a parent on welfare can work or look for work	. . .	. . .	90	85	92
Provide child care and transportation for welfare recipients who work or are in job training or education	77	. . .	. . .	. . .	. . .
Pay transportation/commuting for welfare recipients to get to their jobs	. . .	67	66	. . .	. . .
Provide a job/public sector job if needed	. . .	. . .	60	74	. . .

Attitudes toward Specific Reforms

A major problem with tracking public opinion on proposals for welfare reform is that the terms of the debate among policymakers have shifted so dramatically in the past few years that a long time series does not exist: polltakers tend to ask only about proposals that are under current discussion. And, when confronted with a battery of proposals for policy change about which they may know little, respondents may tend to say that they are in favor of the proposal when they in fact do not have a well-defined opinion at all. This tendency is likely to be particularly strong when the program is one toward which their general opinion is negative, as in the case of welfare.

Public opinion surveys clearly show that while people detest the status quo, they are also hesitant to embrace wholeheartedly some of the proffered alternatives. There is strong support for some changes proposed by the Clinton administration and in the House-passed bill, but uncertainty or strong reservations about others. Although trend data on specific policy options are fragmentary, what do exist suggest that public opinion is still characterized more by ambivalence and stability rather than dramatic change in recent years.

Current reform proposals for welfare can be divided into a few broad categories. *Service approaches* provide subsidized services to welfare recipients to make them more competitive in the job market and ease their transition into the world of work, lessening their dependence on welfare. *Work requirements* force certain categories of recipients to find jobs, take a government-sponsored job, or engage in community service. *Disincentive approaches* try to make welfare less attractive or less available — for example, by excluding teenage mothers from receiving cash benefits, denying additional benefits when a mother already on AFDC conceives an additional child, placing a time limit on receipt of benefits, or limiting eligibility for legal immigrants. *Devolutionary approaches* would allow the states increased flexibility to design their own welfare programs.

Table 6-8. Public Opinion on Work Requirements for Welfare Recipients

Percent in favor of/agreeing with option:

Polling Organization/Sponsor	TMLL for *USNWR*	HT	ABC/ *WP*	CBS/ *NYT*	CBS/ *NYT*	ABC/ *WP*	CBS/ *NYT*	HT for NBC/ *WSJ*
Number surveyed	1,000	1,020	n.a.	. . .	. . .	1,145	1,089	1,504
Month of Poll	11/93	11/93	1/94	1/94	12/94	1/95	4/95	4/95
"Require unemployed fathers of children on welfare to work"	94	. . .	. . .	. . .	. . .	. . .	. . .	. . .
Require fathers of children on welfare to work at public service jobs if they do not pay their child support	91	. . .	. . .	. . .	. . .	. . .	. . .	. . .
Require welfare recipients to work in exchange for their benefits	. . .	. . .	. . .	. . .	. . .	. . .	. . .	95
Limit welfare recipients to a maximum of two years of benefits, after which those who are able to work would have to get a job or do community service	82	. . .	89	. . .	. . .	89	. . .	. . .
Favor work requirements for mothers of preschool children	. . .	60	. . .	. . .	. . .	. . .	. . .	. . .
Favor work requirements for mothers of young children	. . .	. . .	. . .	45	52	. . .	64	. . .
Favor work requirements for single parents with children under three years of age	57	. . .	. . .	. . .	. . .	. . .	. . .	. . .
Favor work requirements for mothers of infants	41	47	. . .	. . .	. . .	. . .	. . .	. . .
Favor work requirement for "any family where the parent has a significant physical or mental disability"	34	. . .	. . .	. . .	. . .	. . .	. . .	. . .

n.a. Not available.

Some service approaches to welfare reform enjoy broad public support. Job training and subsidies for child care receive about 90 percent approval (table 6-7). Two-thirds of respondents support paying transportation costs and providing public sector jobs. The clear public favorite among specific approaches to welfare reform is work requirements which are supported by 90 percent of the public (table 6-8). The public is particularly supportive of work requirements for noncustodial parents who are not paying child support and is most willing to exempt the mothers of very young children from such requirements. But support for applying work requirements even to mothers of young children has increased dramatically in the past year. And as noted earlier, 60 percent of those surveyed claimed that they would be willing to pay more taxes to pay for additional job training and public service employment — a share that remained essentially unchanged from the beginning of 1994 through the spring of 1995 (table 6-4).

Disincentives approaches to reforming welfare enjoy mixed support. Denying an increase in benefits to mothers who bear children while on welfare (known as "family caps") is the most popular (table 6-9). It is supported by three-fifths of the public, although the margin has shrunk slightly since 1993. Only about 25 to 40 percent of respondents (depending on question wording) agree that teenage mothers should be denied access to welfare, another element of the House-passed welfare reform package (softened during floor consideration to allow the provision of vouchers for certain commodities to teenage parents).

Support for exclusion declines if the age of exclusion is raised (table 6-10). However, two-thirds of survey respondents in 1994 supported requiring teenage parents to live with their own parents or another responsible adult rather than setting up their own households if they are to be eligible for welfare benefits. An even greater share — more than 80 percent — favored requiring that a mother report the name of the father before receiving benefits. The public is uneasy, however, by margins of more than two-to-one about proposals to ban benefits to teenage mothers if it means that some of these children might end up in orphanages or foster care.[167] In general, wording of questions that creates an awareness of the welfare of children as well as the mother reduces support for teenage mother exclusions.

The public's ambivalent opinion about welfare is most evident on the matter of time limits for benefits. There is widespread and apparently stable support for the principle of limiting receipt of cash welfare benefits to a few years, with the broadest support for time-limited cash benefits followed by a community service or job requirement (table 6-11). Moreover, a poll taken at the end of 1993 suggests that most people would exempt large portions of the AFDC caseload from a time limit if that limit did not include a job guarantee.[168] Respondents also believe by a three-to-one margin that people should be able to receive benefits as long as they work for them rather than being subject to hard time limits after which no benefits would be received.[169] And when asked in a December 1994 poll what should happen to individuals who hit a time limit, only 10 percent of respondents said that benefits should simply end; more than 81 percent favored a community service requirement or job guarantee instead.[170] Again, the implication is that the public is more concerned with responsible behavior on the part of welfare recipients — in particular engaging in work effort — than with the principle of time limits.

Public opinion on excluding immigrants from eligibility for benefits shows substantial support, but some remaining ambivalence (table 6-12). Support is highest when it is made clear that such a ban would not include those who have become citizens, when benefits are limited to "most" legal immigrants, or when the question specifies that any savings that result from exclusion would be earmarked for paying for job training and child care benefits for welfare reform. The data again suggest that people make distinctions on deservingness within the category of legal immigrants, but may not have well-developed opinions on where those distinctions should be drawn, especially in the case of newly debated issues.

Ambivalence is also evident on turning AFDC decisionmaking over to the states. When asked in a December 1994 poll to choose between experimenting at the state level and reform at the national level, more people chose the state (52 percent) than the national (29 percent), a major shift in support for devolution from the previous year.[171] But in the same poll the public also felt by a 50 percent to 36 percent margin that the federal government should set guidelines for the states rather than allow them complete discretion.

Table 6-9. Public Opinion on Time Limits for Welfare Benefits

Percent in favor of/agreeing with option:

Polling Organization/Sponsor	TMLL for USNWR	HT	ABC/WP	Gallup for CNN/USA Today	LAT	Gallup for CNN/USA Today	CBS/NYT	ABC/WP	YP for Time/CNN	CBS/NYT
Number surveyed	1,000	1,020	n.a.	n.a.	1,682	1,014	n.a.	1,145	800	1,089
Month of Poll	11/93	11/93	1/94	4/94	4/94	12/94	12/94	1/95	3/95	4/95
"Limit welfare benefits to two years and do not allow people to get back on welfare ever"	22	...	...	...	...	...	...	...	...	...
"Limit welfare benefits to five years and do not allow people to get back on welfare for at least five years"	50	...	...	...	...	...	...	...	...	...
"Limit to five years the amount of time a welfare recipient can receive cash payments"	...	...	...	...	...	...	...	...	74	...
"Limit all adults to a total of five years on welfare"	...	...	...	...	...	60	...	...	...	...
"poor mothers should be limited to a maximum of just a few years on welfare . . . ."	...	...	...	...	...	...	...	...	...	61
"After two years, benefits would be ended for all able-bodied recipients, and the government would not provide a job."	...	55	...	...	...	...	...	...	...	...
". . . cut off all benefits to people who had not found a job or become self-sufficient after two years"	...	...	...	67	...	...	...	...	...	...
"Limit welfare recipients to a maximum of two years of benefits, after which those who are able to work would have to get a job or do community service	82	92	89	...	91	...	...	89	...	...
". . . welfare recipients should continue to get benefits as long as they work for them"	...	...	...	...	...	...	71	...	...	...
If benefits cut off after two years, should "government provide separate benefits to the children, even though their parents benefits will have been cut off"	...	...	...	78	...	...	...	...	...	...

Table 6-10. Public Opinion on Family Caps

Percent agreeing with/in favor of proposal

	TMLL for *USNWR*	HT	*LAT*	KRC for Harvard/Kaiser	*NYT/*CBS
Number surveyed	1,000	1,020	1,682	1,200	1,089
Month of poll	11/93	12/93	4/94	12/94	4/95
Stop giving money to mothers if they have another child after they go on welfare (family cap)	65	68	65	59	56

Table 6-11. Public Opinion on Teen Mother Exclusions

Percent believing should not have access/should be denied

Polling organization and sponsor	*LAT*	Gallup for CNN/*USA Today*	*NYT*/CBS	YP for *Time*/CNN	*NYT*/CBS	YP for *Time/*CNN	*NYT/*CBS
Number surveyed	1682	507	4147	800	1190	800	1089
Month of poll	4/94	12/94	12/94	12/94	2/95	3/95	4/95
Deny all benefits to a woman who has a child outside of wedlock [age not specified], even if that would create hardship for the woman and the child	26	...	...	...	...	...	...
"Ending welfare payments to children born of unmarried mothers"	...	36	...	...	...	...	...
"Ending welfare payments to unmarried mothers who have children"	...	40	...	...	...	...	...
Unmarried mothers under the age of 21 who have no way of supporting their children	...	...	20	...	...	...	...
Unmarried mothers under the age of 18	...	...	...	42	...	38	...
Unmarried mothers under the age of 18 who have no way of supporting their children	...	...	...	...	31	...	31
Deny teenage single parents welfare benefits unless they live with parents or another responsible adult	67	...	...	...	...	...	...

Table 6-12. Public Opinion on Benefits for Legal Immigrants

Percent in favor

	TMLL for *USNWR*	Gallup	*LAT*	KRC for Harvard/ Kaiser	YP for *Time/* CNN
Number surveyed	500	. . .	1682	1,200	800
Month of poll	11/93	4/94	4/94	12/94	3/95
"Deny welfare to legal immigrants"	37	. . .	. . .	. . .	. . .
"In order to pay the cost of the job training and child care under welfare reform . . . , deny . . . welfare benefits, with the exception of emergency medical care, to legal immigrants who are not American citizens, even if this would cause such people hardship"	. . .	. . .	54	. . .	. . .
"Government should limit or deny welfare aid to non-citizens. This would include most legal immigrants as well as all illegal immigrants"	. . .	. . .	. . .	64	. . .
"Mak[e] legal immigrants ineligible for most welfare benefits, such as Food Stamps and Medicaid"	. . .	. . .	. . .	. . .	55
"Deny welfare to legal immigrants until they become citizens"	69	. . .	. . .	. . .	. . .
"In order to pay for changes in the welfare system, would you favor or oppose . . . cut all aid to immigrants who have entered the United States legally until they have lived here at least five years"	. . .	69	. . .	. . .	. . .

Who Do You Trust?

There has been far more change in the public's views of who within the federal government they trust to carry out welfare reform than in their views on specific reforms. The Clinton administration came into office with a huge advantage vis-a-vis congressional Republicans in public trust on who would do the best job in carrying out welfare reform (figure 6-2). By the beginning of 1994, however, the administration had squandered most of its advantage as they failed to come forward with a welfare reform plan. Meanwhile, House Republicans did bring out a plan. When the administration finally released its reform proposal in the middle of 1994, their advantage in public trust on welfare had turned into a deficit. And after the 1994 election, it became an immense deficit. Congressional Republicans continued to enjoy a margin of between 10 and 20 points in public trust on handling of welfare matters throughout the House committee and full chamber debate on welfare reform from January through March 1995, perhaps in part because the Clinton administration once again lacked a legislative vehicle of their own. The gap had closed to 6 points again by mid-July 1995 as the administration increased its attacks on the Republicans and the G.O.P. in the Senate became bogged down in disputes over conservative mandates and allocation of block grant funds among the states.

The public's ambivalence about reforming welfare if it means being "too tough on kids" does appear once again in polls focusing on public confidence in political actors to handle the matter, however. For example, a poll released just before the full House of Representatives began debate on welfare reform in March 1995 showed that 51 percent of the public trusted the Republicans in Congress to do a better job than President Clinton of "reforming the welfare system"; 38 percent favored the president. When the issue was framed as "protecting America's children," however, the president was favored over Republicans in Congress by 49 percent to 40 percent. The president's margin of trust over congressional Republicans was even greater in terms of "helping the poor": 61 percent to 27 percent.[172] This ambivalence can also be seen in polls on perceived effects of Republican initiatives when the fate of poor families is mentioned explicitly. Only 12 percent of respondents in an April 1995 survey were concerned that Republican welfare reform initiatives went too far. But in a May 1995 poll 48 percent were more worried that "the Republicans will go too far in denying assistance to poor families" in comparison with 37 percent who thought that "the Democrats will not go far enough in making needed changes in the welfare system."[173]

Figure 6-2. Who Will Do a Better Job of Reforming Welfare: President Clinton or the Republicans in Congress?

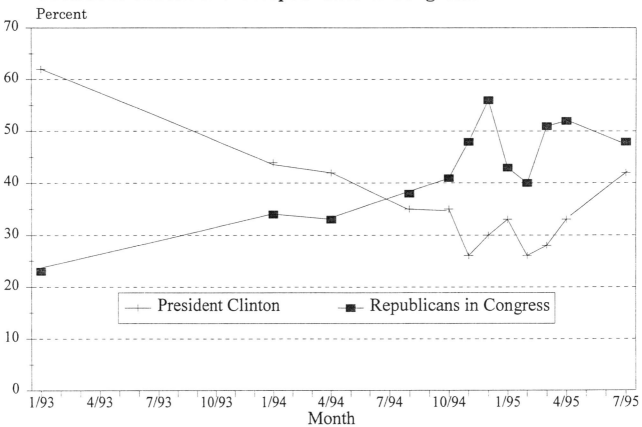

a. The data for December 1994, January 1995, and April 1995 are the average of multiple polls conducted during those months.

Conclusions and Implications

Public opinion toward welfare reform has shown both remarkable continuity and important elements of change in recent years. The most fundamental and durable characteristics of American public opinion toward recipients of and programs for low-income families are an ambivalence toward the dual clienteles of those programs and a deep dislike of the programs themselves, especially AFDC. The public wants to protect children. The public also wants parents to behave in a responsible manner, which it defines primarily in terms of parents working or preparing for work, mothers not having more children while they are on welfare, and noncustodial fathers paying child support. They dislike the welfare system because it fails to produce these outcomes.

Beyond these points of near consensus, there is division, a lack of unqualified positions — and much hope that political leaders will design programs that remedy identifiable problems with the welfare system. People hope that welfare reform will save money, for example, but they are willing to spend more money for a program that reduces dependency. If their leaders tell them that a particular course of welfare reform can be accomplished that will promote responsibility and protect children, people are inclined to accept that judgement — until they are reminded about relevant additional considerations.[174]

There has been some change in attitudes, notably an increase in the number of people who think that too much is being spent on welfare, that the poor are primarily responsible for their own condition, and that work should be required for mothers of young children. It is difficult to be certain how stable those changes will be, however, since they could have several causes. They may result from a permanent conversion in attitudes resulting from the recent welfare debate, temporary changes in attitude resulting from the fact that Republican voices dominated the welfare debate in the first half of 1995, or temporary cyclical changes, since support for welfare spending and welfare programs tends to grow as welfare spending decreases. Moreover, looking at trends in poll results in the past year suggests that despite a ferocious public debate and passage of a very bold bill by the House of Representatives, public opinion has been surprisingly stable on most specific reform proposals. Work and training requirements remain the core concerns where public support is widespread. Public opinion has not coalesced — at least not yet — around most of the conservative mandates in the House welfare reform bill; many of them (for example, excluding coverage for teenage mothers) remain highly controversial.

The 1994 election results suggested anew the possibility of a partisan realignment in the United States. The implications for a realignment of public attitudes on welfare reform are necessarily speculative. Political realignment involves major issues, and generally involves not a massive change of opinion in the entire electorate, but rather a change within particular segments of the electorate. Detecting shifts in public opinion that might presage such a realignment thus requires a much more finely grained analysis of the preferences of particular segments of the electorate than has been attempted here. Clearly presidential candidate Clinton believed that giving the Democratic party a new image vis à vis welfare would provide an opportunity to counteract the hemorrhage of working class whites from the party. Journalist Mickey Kaus argued after the 1994 election that the administration's failure to move more swiftly to develop and pass a welfare reform package in the first two years of its term was "the fundamental strategic mistake of the Clinton presidency. . . . If President Clinton had pushed for welfare reform rather than health care reform in 1994, we would now be talking about a great Democratic realignment, rather than a great Republican realignment."[175]

This interpretation is plausible, but it is difficult to see welfare alone as a realigning issue independent of the public's suspicion or dread of big, centralized, ineffective government; or independent of the politics of social inequality. As a realigning issue, welfare may be less like the Great Depression as a *crisis* issue in the 1930s than like race as an evolving issue in the 1960s.[176]

Although discontent with current welfare policies and belief in personal responsibility for economic failure may be at historic highs, the fundamental ambivalence of the public on many specific welfare-related policy proposals remains. Rather than leading to and solidifying a realignment, welfare issues are more likely to prevent the solidification of any existing or new realignment because they allow both sides of the partisan divide to call up and reinforce unfavorable attitudes that the electorate has about the other party: Democrats' coddling of the shiftless and irresponsible and Republicans' favoring the rich and unwillingness to aid the helpless.

Notes

1. *Welfare Transformation Act of 1995*, H. Rept. 104-81, pt. 1, 104 Cong. 1 sess. (GPO, March 15, 1995), p. 24; and S. 1120, *Work Opportunity Act of 1995*, 104 Cong. 1 sess., creating a new section 411 of the Social Security Act.

2. In the House bill, states can choose to have their funding allocation based on the average of their fiscal year 1992-94 allocations.

3. States are required to cover pregnant women and children under age 6 with family incomes below 133 percent of the federal poverty standard and children under age 18 born after September 30, 1983, with family incomes below 100 percent of the poverty standard. States are also required to continue Medicaid coverage for a defined period to some families who lose AFDC eligibility because of increased income or hours of employment. Optional coverage groups include pregnant women and infants with incomes between 133 and 185 percent of the federal poverty standard and medically needy persons who do not meet the income and asset tests of categorical income transfer programs. For details on mandatory and optional coverage groups and services in Medicaid, see *1994 Green Book: Overview of Entitlement Programs: Background Material and Data on Programs within the Jurisdiction of the Committee on Ways and Means*, Committee Print, House Committee on Ways and Means, 103 Cong. 2 sess. (Government Printing Office, 1994), pp. 783-89.

4. Even a waiver approach using a control group and random assignment methodology is not without serious limitations for evaluation purposes. Two critical problems have been noted by Michael Wiseman in his discussion of the AFDC program. First, waivers often incorporate a number of different program changes applied simultaneously to the same population; as a result, it is often impossible to know which of several program variations produced any measured effect. Second, this evaluation method is inappropriate for testing program changes that depend for their impact on engendering altered expectations and practices — for example, expectations about the availability of AFDC benefits for teenagers who become pregnant. The first problem suggests that some innovations be tested individually rather than in groups; the second suggests that some careful evaluations of entire states, using states that are as similar as possible except for the treated policy change as the control group, may be a more appropriate evaluative technique for some policy experiments. See Michael Wiseman, "Evaluation: Lessons from the Welfare Waiver Demos," paper presented at the Institute for Research on Poverty Forum on Welfare Block Grants: Advantages and Disadvantages, February 1995.

5. The General Accounting Office reported that in "nine block grants, from fiscal years 1983 and 1991, the Congress added new cost ceilings and set-asides or changed existing ones 58 times." See *Block Grants: Characteristics, Experience, and Lessons Learned*, report HEHS-95-74 (February 1995), p. 11. See also General Accounting

Office, *Block Grants: Increases in Set-Asides and Cost Ceilings since 1982*, report HRD-92-58 (July 1992).

6.   For an application of these tactics to the AFDC program, see Paul E. Peterson and Mark Rom, *Welfare Magnets: A New Case for a National Standard* (Brookings, 1990).

7.   *1994 Green Book*, p. 378.

8.   R. Kent Weaver, *Automatic Government: The Politics of Indexation* (Brookings, 1988), chap. 5.

9.   Helen F. Ladd and Fred C. Doolittle, "Which Level of Government Should Assist the Poor?," *National Tax Journal*, vol. 35 (September 1982), pp. 323-36.

10. See Wayne Vroman, "Rainy Day Funds: Contingency Funding for Welfare Block Grants," in Isabel V. Sawhill, eds., *Welfare Reform: An Analysis of the Issues* (Washington: Urban Institute, 1995), pp. 11-14.

11. A GAO study notes that of the nine block grants created by the Omnibus Reconciliation Act of 1981, three of them — Community Services, Maternal and Child Health Services, and Preventive Health and Health Services — are "still largely tied to 1981 allocations" rather than changing to reflect changes in population, need, and fiscal capacity. General Accounting Office, *Block Grants: Characteristics, Experience, and Lessons Learned*, p. 9.

12. The House-passed bill also allows states to build up unexpended balances from their block grant to use during recessions. But because the block grant does not have matching requirements, this could only occur if states choose to expend some state dollars while allowing federal dollars to build up, or if they reduce their total family support expenditures below the level of their federal block grant allocations. The former is extremely unlikely, and the latter would require either an implausibly successful welfare-to-work transition or a very severe race to the bottom in eligibility and benefits.

13. Wayne Vroman has estimated an economic peak-to-trough increase of 10.5 percent in the 1989 AFDC caseload. See Vroman, "Rainy Day Funds."

14. See Center on Budget and Policy Priorities, *An Analysis of the Proposed Rainy Day Fund* (Washington, 1995), for a more detailed discussion of the problems posed by triggers and funding ceilings in the Rainy Day Fund.

15. On the Unemployment Insurance experience after 1981, see Vroman, "Rainy Day Funds"; Vroman, "The Aggregate Performance on Unemployment Insurance, 1980-85," in W. Lee Hansen and James F. Byers, eds., *Unemployment Insurance: The Second Half-Century* (Madison, Wisc.: University of Wisconsin Press, 1990), pp. 19-46; and Advisory Council on Unemployment Compensation, *Report and Recommendations*, Washington,D.C.: The Council, February 1994, and Advisory Council on Unemployment Compensation, *Unemployment Insurance in the United*

States: Benefits, Financing, Coverage, Washington, D.C.: The Council, February 1995.

16.   Sonenstein and Acs argue that recent increases in overall teenage birthrates may be partially the result of an increased number of Hispanic teenagers, who have teenage birthrates comparable to those of blacks, relative to the population of non-Hispanic whites, who have lower teenage birthrates. See Freya L. Sonenstein and Gregory L. Acs, "Teenage Childbearing: The Trends and their Implications," in Isabel V. Sawhill, ed., *Welfare Reform: An Analysis of the Issues* (Washington: Urban Institute, 1995), pp. 47-50.

17.   Robert Moffitt, "Incentive Effects of the U.S. Welfare System: A Review," *Journal of Economic Literature*, vol. 30 (March 1992), pp. 1-61.

18.   See Gregory Acs, "The Impact of AFDC on Young Women's Childbearing Decisions," Unpublished manuscript, (Urban Institute, 1994); Chong-Bum An, Robert Haveman, and Barbara Wolfe, "The Effect of Childhood Events and Economic Circumstances on Teen Fertility Out-of-Wedlock and the Receipt of Welfare: Estimates from a Sequential Decision Model," Paper presented at Meetings of Population Association of America, Toronto, 1990; Greg J. Duncan and Saul D. Hoffman, "Welfare Benefits, Economic Opportunities, and Out-of-Wedlock Births among Black Teenage Girls" *Demography*, vol. 27 (November 1990), pp. 519-35; David T. Ellwood and Mary Jo Bane, "The Impact of AFDC on Family Structure and Living Arrangements," *Research in Labor Economics*, vol. 7 (1985), pp. 137-207; Shelly Lundberg and Robert Plotnick, "Effects of State Welfare, Abortion, and Family Planning Policies on Premarital Childbearing among White Adolescents," *Family Planning Perspectives*, vol. 22, no. 6 (1990), pp. 246-51, 275; Charles Murray, "Welfare and the Family: The U.S. Experience," *Journal of Labor Economics*, vol. 11, no. 1 (1993), pp. S224-S262; Robert Plotnick, "Welfare and Out-of-Wedlock Childbearing: Evidence from the 1980s," *Journal of Marriage and the Family*, vol. 52 (August 1990), pp. 735-46; Mark R. Rank, "Fertility Among Women on Welfare: Incidence and Determinants," *American Sociological Review*, vol. 54 (April 1989), pp. 296-304; Philip K. Robins and Paul Fronstin, "Welfare Benefits and Family-Size Decisions of Never-Married Women," Institute for Research on Poverty Discussion Paper 1022-93, University of Wisconsin, 1993; Washington State Institute for Public Policy, *Women in Transition: A Family Income Study Newsletter* (Olympia, Wash.: Evergreen State College, September 1993); C.R. Winegarden, "AFDC and Illegitimacy Ratios: A Vector-Autoregressive Model," *Applied Economics*, vol. 20 (December 1988), pp. 1589-1601.

19.   For a good summary of both the facts and the potential causes of the changes in wages for less-skilled men, see Frank Levy and Richard Murnane, "U.S. Earnings Levels and Earnings Inequality: A Review of Recent Trends and Explanations," *Journal of Economic Literature*, vol. 30, no. 3 (1992), pp. 1333-81. For a discussion of the implications of these trends in the low-wage labor market, see Demetra Smith Nightingale and Robert H. Haveman, eds., *The Work Alternative: Welfare Reform and the Realities of the Job Market*, (Washington, DC: The Urban Institute Press, 1995).

20.   McLanahan and Sandefur document the problems faced by children of all ages who grow up in a single-parent family. See Sara McLanahan and Gary Sandefur, *Growing Up with a Single Parent: What Hurts, What Helps* (Cambridge, Mass.: Harvard University Press, 1994).

21.   See Judith S. Musick, *Young, Poor, and Pregnant* (New Haven, Conn.: Yale University Press, 1993) on the problems and pressures that low-income teenage women often face as they struggle to cope with their own adolescence at the same time they are also coping with motherhood.

22.   Evidence on children in single-parent families is in Sara McLanahan and Gary Sandefur, *Growing Up with a Single Parent: What Hurts, What Helps*. Evidence on children in poverty is found in Jane E. Miller and Sanders Korenman, "Poverty and Children's Nutritional Status in the U.S.," *American Journal of Epidemiology*, vol. 140, no. 3 (August 1994), pp. 233-42; Sanders Korenman, Jane E. Miller and John E. Sjaastad, "Long-term Poverty and Child Development in the U.S.: Results from the NLSY," *Children and Youth Services Review*, vol. 17 (January 1995), pp. 127-55; and Irwin Garfinkel and Sara McLanahan, "Single-Mother Families, Economic Insecurity, and Government Policy," in *Confronting Poverty*, Sheldon H. Danziger, Gary D. Sandefure, and Daniel H. Weinberg, eds. (Cambridge, Mass.: Harvard University Press, 1994).

23.   See Arline T. Geronimus and Sanders Korenman, "The Socioeconomic Consequences of Teen Childbearing Reconsidered," *Quarterly Journal of Economics*, vol. 107 (1992), pp. 1187-1214; Arline T. Geronimus and Sanders Korenman, "The Socioeconomic Costs of Teenage Childbearing: Evidence and Interpretation," *Demography*, vol. 30, no. 2 (1993), pp. 281-96; and Saul D. Hoffman, E. Michael Foster, and Frank F. Furstenberg, Jr., "Reevaluating the Costs of Teenage Childbearing," *Demography*, vol. 30, no. 1 (1993), pp. 1-13.

24.   V. Joseph Hotz, Susan Williams McElroy, and Seth G. Sanders, "The Costs and Consequences of Teenage Childbearing for Mothers," Irving B. Harris Graduate School of Public Policy Working Paper Series, 95-1, 1995.

25.   For additional information on movement on and off the welfare rolls see LaDonna Ann Pavetti, "The Dynamics of Welfare and Work: Exploring the Process by Which Young Women Work Their Way off Welfare," Ph.D. dissertation, Harvard University, 1993; Rebecca M. Blank and Patricia Ruggles, "Short-term Recidivism among Public-Assistance Recipients," *American Economic Review*, vol. 84 (May 1994), pp. 49-53; Kathleen Mullan Harris, "Work and Welfare among Single Mothers in Poverty," *American Journal of Sociology*, vol. 99 (September 1993), pp. 317-52; and Gregory C. Weeks, "Leaving Public Assistance in Washington State," Working Paper, Washington State Institute for Public Policy, Evergreen State College, April 1991.

26.   For a much more detailed explanation of this issue, see Mary Jo Bane and David T. Ellwood, *Welfare Realities: From Rhetoric to Reform* (Cambridge, Mass.: Harvard University Press, 1994).

27. The older research used data that reported AFDC participation only at any time during an entire year. See Bane and Ellwood, *Welfare Realities: From Rhetoric to Reform*. More recent work examines participation on a month-by-month basis and allows the identification of short spells of nonreceipt within a year. See Pavetti, "Dynamics of Welfare and Work."

28. Harris, "Work and Welfare among Single Mothers in Poverty"; Pavetti, "Dynamics of Welfare and Work"; and Weeks, "Leaving Public Assistance in Washington State."

29. James Riccio, Daniel Friedlander, and Stephen Freedman, *GAIN: Benefits, Costs, and Three-Year Impacts of a Welfare-to-Work Program* (New York: Manpower Demonstration Research Corporation, September 1994).

30. Lynn Olson, Linnea Berg, and Aimee Conrad, "High Job Turnover among the Urban Poor: The Project Match Experience" (Evanston, Ill.: Center for Urban Affairs and Policy Research, 1990).

31. There were 10,652,307 recipients in 1972 and 10,689,249 in 1989. All numbers on AFDC caseloads and recipients come from *Green Book*, various years.

32. One such rule was the prohibition against having a man in the house. See David T. Ellwood, *Poor Support: Poverty in the American Family* (Basic Books, 1988), p. 37-38, and R. Shep Melnick, *Between the Lines: Interpreting Welfare Rights* (Brookings, 1994).

33. All figures have been adjusted for inflation and are stated in 1994 dollars.

34. The components of the sum are the AFDC and Food Stamp benefit for a family of four with no other income and the insurance value of Medicaid. The insurance value of Medicaid is calculated by multiplying the average Medicaid expenditure for an AFDC family of four by the ratio of AFDC families with Medicaid expenditures to the total number of AFDC families.

35. For example, see Thomas Gabe, "Demographic Trends Affecting Aid to Families with Dependent Children (AFDC) Caseload Growth," Congressional Research Service, 93-7 EPW, December 1992.

36. The basic caseload excludes two-parent families receiving AFDC under the Unemployed Parent program.

37. The number of families headed by a never-married mother increased 23 percent between 1989 and 1993, but it increased 33 percent between 1985 and 1989, 25 percent between 1981 and 1985, and 42 percent between 1977 and 1981.

38. Compare that with the increase in the value of Medicaid of about $115 a month over the same period. The JOBS benefit maximum of $37 a month is calculated by doubling the total authorized federal spending on JOBS of $1.1 billion. (The minimum federal match rate for any aspect of the program is 50 percent; average

match rates are much higher.) This figure is then divided by caseload times 12 months. Considerably more is spent per recipient of JOBS benefits, but access to the program is limited and benefits per welfare recipient is probably a better estimate of expected benefits.

39.   U.S. Department of Justice, *Drugs, Crime, and the Justice System: A National Report* (1984).

40.   For drug-related crime, see Scott Boggess, "Did Criminal Activity Increase during the 1980s? Comparisons across Data Sources," Working Paper 4431 (Cambridge, Mass.: National Bureau of Economic Research, 1993), fig. 8. For cocaine use, see General Accounting Office, *Health Consequences and Treatment for Crack Abuse*, HRD-91-55FS, p. 11.

41.   Most studies find notable effects of benefit generosity on welfare caseloads. See Robert Moffitt, "Incentive Effects of the U.S. Welfare System: A Review," pp. 1-61.

42.   Michelle Ruess, "N.J. Would Avert Welfare Cutoff," *Bergen (N.J.) Record* April 13, 1995.

43.   Washington State Institute for Public Policy, *Women in Transition: A Family Income Study Newsletter*, (Olympia, WA: Evergreen State College, September 1993).

44.   U.S. Department of Health and Human Services and U.S. Department of Agriculture, *H.R. 4: The Personal Responsibility Act of 1995: Preliminary Impacts, Summary and State by State Analysis*, April 7, 1995, p. 3.

45.   Ruess, "N.J. Would Avert Welfare Cutoff."

46.   June O'Neill, "Report of Dr. June O'Neill."

47.   See O'Neill, "Report of Dr. June O'Neill," and State of New Jersey, Department of Human Services, press release, May 16, 1995.

48.   Correspondence between Michael Camasso, principal investigator, and Rudolf Myers, assistant director, Division of Family Development, June 14, 1995, released by HHS.

49.   Both drops are measured relative to the fertility rate in the equivalent six months in the year before the cap was put into effect.

50.   Although the fertility rates of those subject to the cap and those exempt from it are virtually the same, one could not reject the statistical hypothesis that the cap has lowered birth rates among those subject to the cap by 10 percent, but that random factors having to do with who was chosen for the experimental groups result in measured birth rates. Calculations by the author from a table provided by HHS.

51. See Judith Havemann, "Abortion Rate Increased Under N.J. 'Family Cap'," *Washington Post*, May 17, 1995, p. A15, and Iver Petersen, "Abortions Up Slightly for Welfare Mothers," *New York Times*, May 17, 1995, p. B7.

52. See, for example Hilary Hoynes, "Does Welfare Play Any Role in Female Headship Decisions?" National Bureau of Economic Research Working Paper 5149 (Cambridge, Mass.: June 1995); "Welfare Benefits, Economic Opportunities, and Out-of-Wedlock Births among Black Teenage Girls," *Demography*, vol. 27 (1990), David Ellwood and Mary Jo Bane, "The Impact of AFDC on Family Structure and Living Arrangements," in *Research in Labor Economics*, vol. 7 (1985); Charles Murray, "Welfare and the Family: The U.S. Experience"; George R. G. Clarke and Robert P. Strauss, "Children as Income Producing Assets: The Case of Teen Illegitimacy and Government Transfers," Rochester mimeo, August 1994; Gregory Acs, "The Impact of AFDC on Young Women's Childbearing Decisions," Discussion Paper 1011-93, Institute for Research on Poverty, Discussion paper 1011-93, August 1993; Douglas E. Hyatt and William J. Milne, "Can Public Policy Affect Fertility?" *Canadian Public Policy*, vol. 12 (1991); and Philip K. Robins and Paul Fronstin, "Welfare Benefits and Family Size Decisions of Never Married Women," Discussion Paper 1022-93, Institute for Research on Poverty, September 1993.

53. See Gary Burtless, "The Effect of Reform on Employment, Earnings, and Income," in Phoebe H. Cottingham and David T. Ellwood, eds., *Welfare Policy for the 1990s* (Cambridge, Mass.: Harvard University Press, 1989), pp. 103-45; Congressional Budget Office, *Work-Related Programs for Welfare Recipients* (April 1987); Daniel Friedlander and Gary Burtless, *Five Years After: The Long-Term Effects of Welfare-to-Work Programs* (New York: Russell Sage, 1995); Judith M. Gueron and Edward Pauly, *From Welfare to Work* (New York: Russell Sage, 1991); and Riccio, Friedlander, and Freedman, *GAIN*.

54. See Gary Burtless, "The Employment Prospects of Welfare Recipients," in Demetra Smith Nightingale and Robert H. Haveman, eds., *The Work Alternative: Welfare Reform and the Realities of the Job Market* (Washington, DC: Urban Institute Press, 1995), pp. 71-106.

55. See Riccio and others, *GAIN*.

56. See Howard S. Bloom and others, *The National JTPA Study: Title IIA Impacts on Earnings and Employment at 18 Months* (Bethesda, Md.: Abt Associates, 1993); Burtless, "The Effect of Reform on Employment, Earnings, and Income"; Burtless, "The Employment Prospects of Welfare Recipients"; and Gueron and Pauly, *From Welfare to Work*.

57. See Manpower Demonstration Research Corporation, Board of Directors *Summary and Findings of the National Supported Work Demonstration* (Cambridge, Mass.: Ballinger, 1980); Burtless, "The Effect of Reform on Employment, Earnings, and Income"; John H. Enns, Kathleen L. Flanagan, and Stephen H. Bell, *AFDC Homemaker-Home Aide Demonstration: Trainee Employment and Earnings* (Cambridge, Mass.: Abt Associates, 1986); Gueron and Pauly, *From Welfare to*

Work; and Larry L. Orr, *AFDC Homemaker-Home Health Aide Demonstrations: Benefits and Costs* (Cambridge, Mass.: Abt Associates, 1986).

58. If the community service performed by participants is highly valued by nonparticipants, the social cost of workfare schemes might be very low, of course. Ordinarily, however, it is very difficult to place a dollar value on the services performed. If the services were highly valued by taxpayers, it is likely that they would be willing to have them performed by paid public employees or private contractors.

59. See Gary Burtless, "When Work Doesn't Work: Employment Programs for Welfare Recipients," *Brookings Review*, vol. 10 (Spring 1992), pp. 26-29; and Gueron and Pauly, *Welfare to Work*.

60. See Bloom and others, *The National JTPA Study*.

61. See Gary Burtless, "Are Targeted Wage Subsidies Harmful? Evidence from a Wage Voucher Experience," *Industrial and Labor Relations Review*, vol. 39 (October 1985), pp. 105-14.

62. See Burtless, "Are Targeted Wage Subsidies Harmful? Evidence from a Wage Voucher Experience."

63. LaDonna Pavetti, "Who Is Affected by Time Limits?" in Sawhill, ed., *Welfare Reform: An Analysis of the Issues*, p. 33.

64. Rebecca A. Maynard, "Subsidized Employment and Non-Labor Market Alternatives for Welfare Recipients," in Nightingale and Haveman, eds., *The Work Alternative*, p. 112.

65. Riccio and others, *GAIN*, p. 18.

66. Friedlander and Burtless, *Five Years After*, p. 88.

67. Riccio and others, *GAIN*, p. 122.

68. *Statistical Abstract of the United States, 1994* (Bureau of the Census, 1994), p. 402.

69. Nicholas Zill, Kristin Moore, and T. Stief, *Welfare Mothers as Potential Employees: A Statistical Profile Based on National Survey Data* (Washington, DC: Child Trends, 1991), cited in Maynard, "Subsidized Employment," p. 116.

70. Daniel Friedlander and others, *Arkansas: Final Report on the WORK Program in Two Counties* (New York: Manpower Demonstration Research Corporation, September 1995).

71. Riccio, Friedlander, and Freedman, *GAIN*.

72. Riccio, Friedlander, and Freedman, *GAIN*, p. 166.

73. James J. Kemple and Joshua Haimson, *Florida's Project Independence: Program Implementation, Participation Patterns, and First-Year Impacts* (New York: Manpower Demonstration Research Corporation, January 1994).

74. Kemple and Haimson, *Florida's Project Independence*, p. 105.

75. See David T. Ellwood, *Poor Support: Poverty and the American Family* (Basic Books, 1988).

76. The exemption is 10 percent of the caseload in the House bill and 15 percent in the Senate bill.

77. Tabulations by Rebecca Blank using the March 1994 current population survey.

78. See Pavetti, "Who Is Affected by Time Limits?"

79. General Accounting Office, *An Evaluation of the 1981 AFDC Changes: Final Report*, GAO/PEMD-85-4 (July 2, 1985), p. iv.

80. See Sandra K. Danziger and Sheldon Danziger, "Will Welfare Recipients Find Work When Welfare Ends?," in Sawhill, ed., *Welfare Reform: An Analysis of the Issues*, pp. 41-44.

81. Alaska and Hawaii are the two most generous states. All benefit figures are from 1993, the most recent year for which published data are available. *1994 Green Book*, pp. 391-92, provides data on average monthly payments.

82. The federal "matching rate" for each state is contained in *1994 Green Book*, pp. 383-84. In 1994 the federal government share of benefits varied from 50 to 79 percent.

83. It has been reported that Connecticut Governor John G. Rowland has proposed "the toughest eligibility requirements in the country to discourage poor people from moving there." Dirk Johnson, "Large Benefits Lure Chicagoans to Wisconsin," *New York Times*, May 8, 1995, p. A11.

84. In 1985 there were at least thirty-two significant regulations affecting welfare eligibility that varied from state to state. On an eligibility permissiveness index, with a scale from 0 (restrictive) to 100 (permissive), the average state scored 47, the most restrictive state scored 28, and the most permissive state scored 75. The correlation between permissiveness and benefits was 0.67. Paul E. Peterson and Mark C. Rom, "The Case for a National Welfare Standard," *Brookings Review*, vol. 6 (Winter 1988), pp. 24-32.

85. *1994 Green Book*, pp. 375-77, provides data on maximum AFDC benefits in the states since 1970.

86. *1994 Green Book*, pp. 366-67.

87.   Edward M. Gramlich and Deborah S. Laren, "Migration and Income Redistribution Responsibilities," *Journal of Human Resources*, vol. 19 (Fall 1983), pp. 489-511; Rebecca M. Blank, "The Effect of Welfare and Wage Levels on the Location Decisions of Female-Headed Households," *Journal of Urban Economics*, vol. 24 (September 1988), pp. 186-211; Paul Peterson and Mark Rom, "American Federalism, Welfare Policy, and Residential Choices," *American Political Science Review* vol. 83 (September 1989), pp. 711-28; and Rebecca Clark, "Does Welfare Affect Migration?" (Urban Institute, Washington, DC, 1990).

88.   Russell L. Hanson and John T. Hartman, "Do Welfare Magnets Attract?" Institute for Research on Poverty, Madison, Wisc., 1994; and James R. Walker, "Migration among Low-Income Households: Helping the Witch Doctors Reach Consensus," Institute for Research on Poverty, Madison, Wisc., 1994.

89.   Moffitt, "Incentive Effects on the U.S. Welfare System: A Review"; and Thomas Corbett, "The Wisconsin Welfare Magnet Debate: What Is an Ordinary Member of the Tribe to Do When the Witch Doctors Disagree?" *Focus*, vol. 13 (Fall and Winter 1991), pp. 19-28.

90.   In 1969 the Supreme Court ruled (in *Shapiro* v. *Thompson*) that denying benefits to new residents was unconstitutional.

91.   Waiver applications by Illinois and Wyoming to create two-tier systems have been denied. Other states have expressed interest in establishing such systems but are waiting to submit formal applications until the legal status of two-tier systems becomes clearer. Phone interview, Peter Germanis, program analysis officer, Administration on Children and Families, Department of Health and Human Services, May 19, 1995.

92.   The U.S. Supreme Court let stand a 1993 ruling by the Minnesota Supreme Court (*Mitchell* v. *Steffen*) that overturned legislation creating a two-tier system in that state. A federal judge has ruled the California two-tier system unconstitutional; it is now before the U.S. Supreme Court. The Wisconsin two-tier system is also undergoing judicial review.

93.   Personal Responsibility Act of 1995, H.R. 4, sec. 101, modifying sec. 403(c)(2) of the Social Security Act.

94.   For example, California officials estimate that their two-tier system would have saved 0.4 percent of its AFDC budget in 1993 ($22 million out of $6 billion). Antonio Olivio, "Comments on Welfare Laws Run Gamut," *Los Angeles Times*, January 20, 1995, p. B3.

95.   The number of AFDC recipients entering high-benefit states must exactly equal the number of recipients leaving low-benefit states. A very few people who move to high-benefit states may not remain on AFDC as long if interstate competition causes benefits to be reduced in those states.

96. Because welfare is, at most, only one of the many factors that influence migration, the effect of this change would likely be too small to measure accurately.

97. The bills raise to 50 percent (from the current 20 percent) the proportion of single parents that must participate in work or work programs (by fiscal year 2001 in the Senate Finance bill and 2003 in the House bill). They raise to 90 percent (from the current 50 percent) the participation rate for family heads in two-parent households. States that fail to meet annual participation quotas as they rise to new levels will be subject to fiscal sanctions of up to 5 percent of their block grants. States also will be barred from using federal dollars to assist recipients at any point after they reach a five-year lifetime limit for receiving welfare. The House bill permits states to give exemptions to 10 percent of families reaching the time limit. The Senate Finance bill allows exemptions for 15 percent.

98. The Congressional Budget Office (CBO) estimates that the freeze on block grant appropriations would reduce federal funds below expected levels by $600,000 in 1996 and by $2.6 billion in the year 2002. John Tapogna and Sheila Dacey, "Illustrative Estimates of Training and Child Care Costs Required in the Senate and House Versions of H.R. 4," memorandum of the Congressional Budget Office, June 26, 1995.

99. In Riverside, 23 percent of program participants and 18.4 percent of nonparticipants in an experimental control group were employed and off welfare at the end of the program's third year, a difference of 4.6 percent. Evidence indicates that a substantial proportion of recipients who leave welfare for work do not remain permanently employed. For a discussion of findings on the effects of work programs, see chapter 3 in this volume.

100. Riverside's program made greater use of job search and mandatory participation; Alameda's utilized more education and voluntary participation. For a full discussion, see James Riccio, Daniel Friedlander and Stephen Freedman, *GAIN: Benefits, Costs, and Three-Year Impacts of a Welfare-to-Work Program*, pp. xxvii and xxxii.

101. The difficulties of singling out specific aspects of casework practice and their consequences for outcomes are evident in even a cursory review of available data. For example, among the counties included in the MDRC experiment, Los Angeles had the highest proportion of participants ever facing conciliation or sanctions (34.2%). It also produced the lowest impacts on a variety of measures of effectiveness. Riverside — a program demonstrating greater effectiveness — had the second highest proportion of participants facing conciliation or sanctions (33.9%). However, even in Riverside fewer than 7% of participants were actually sanctioned. (Riccio *et al.*, p. 60)

Because of methodological flaws, studies that have purported to demonstrate the benefits of "tough" casework practices have been misleading. For example, a recent report on a program in Kenosha, Wisconsin based its conclusions about the effectiveness of "authoritative" casework largely on the unvalidated claims of the program's managers. It did not directly examine agency practice, test for the significance of variations in practice, or measure program effectiveness in improving earnings or employment. See Lawrence M. Mead, "The New Paternalism in Action: Welfare Reform in Wisconsin," draft manuscript, January 1995.

Other analyses, although inconclusive, have offered evidence indicating that supportive models of casework practice are most beneficial. See Olivia Golden, *Poor Children and Welfare Reform: Executive Summary of the Final Report* (New York: Foundation for Child Development, 1991); Toby Herr and Suzanne L. Wagner, "A Long-Term, Developmental View of Leaving Welfare: The Project Match Experience," Chicago: Erikson Institute, working draft, April 1995; Alan Hershey, *The Minority Female Single Parent Demonstration: Program Operations*, Technical Report to the Rockefeller Foundation, (New York: Mathematica Policy Research, 1988). Until more systematic research on alternative casework approaches is available, states should be cautious about making wholesale changes in agency practice.

102. Irene Lurie and Jan L. Hagen, *Implementing JOBS: The Initial Design and Structure of Local Programs* (Albany, N.Y.: Rockefeller Institute of Government, July 1993), p. 33.

103. A recent Columbia University study in Harlem found a ratio of fourteen job seekers for each new job opening in fast food restaurants. Katherine Newman, "What Inner-City Jobs for Welfare Moms?" *New York Times*, May 20, 1995, p. A23. The entry of new job seekers may also depress wages in some sectors of the labor market. See Gary Burtless, "Employment Prospects of Welfare Recipients."

104. These problems are noted in the following reports: Evelyn Z. Brodkin, "The State Side of the Welfare Contract: Discretion and Accountability in Policy Delivery." SSA Working Paper #5, Chicago: The University of Chicago, forthcoming; Lurie and Hagen, *Implementing JOBS: The Initial Design and Structure of Local Programs*; and Irene Lurie and Jan Hagen, *Implementing JOBS: Progress and Promise*, Albany, N.Y.: Rockefeller Institute, August 1994.

105. See James Kemple, Daniel Friedlander, and Veronica Fellerath, *Florida's Project Independence: Benefits, Costs and Two-Year Impacts of Florida's JOBS Program* (New York: MDRC, 1995).

106. Lurie and Hagen (1994) found that agencies were unable to secure legislative approval for staffing increases even when staff shortages were perceived as hindering the ability to meet participation rates (pp. 21-25). Block grants that eliminate dollar for dollar federal cost-sharing of administrative expenses would increase the marginal cost to states of providing administrative resources.

107. Olivia Golden, *Poor Children and Welfare Reform: Executive Summary of the Final Report*; Toby Herr and Suzanne L. Wagner, "A Long-Term, Developmental View of Leaving Welfare: The Project Match Experience," Chicago: Erikson Institute, April 1995; and Alan Hershey, *The Minority Female Single Parent Demonstration: Program Operations*, p. 156.

108.   See Riccio *et al.* (1994) for the results of the Riverside County case management study.

109.   In their ten-state study, Lurie and Hagen, *Implementing JOBS*, found that "administrators and staff in the majority of states were concerned about the availability of jobs for participants within their states or within certain areas of the states" (p. 230). They and others have pointed to the importance of skilled job developers in creating concrete job opportunities for welfare recipients in a variety of agency settings. According to one program evaluator: "it is critical that the training organization be represented to the employer community by experienced, credible placement staff. Placement must be a stable and permanent function of the organization, conducted by a staff who, over time, can develop their own personal reputations with employers, as well as the reputation of the organization as a whole." Alan Hershey, *The Minority Female Single Parent Demonstration: Program Operations*, p. 156.

110.   Evelyn Z. Brodkin, *The False Promise of Administrative Reform: Implementing Quality Control in Welfare* (Philadelphia, Penn.: Temple University Press, 1986); Frederica Kramer, *From Quality Control to Quality Improvement in AFDC and Medicaid* (Washington, DC: National Academy Press, 1988).

111.   These types of activities have been documented by analysts in a variety of agencies and welfare programs. See, for example, Brodkin, "The State Side of the Welfare Contract" (forthcoming); Yeheskel Hasenfeld, "The Role of Employment Placement Services in Maintaining Poverty," *Social Service Review*, (1975); Lois M. Quinn, *Procedures for Determining School Absences Under the Wisconsin Learnfare Policy* (University of Wisconsin Employment and Training Institute, Milwaukee, April 1995); U.S. Government Accounting Office, *CWEP's Implementation Results to Date Raise Questions About the Administration's Proposed Mandatory Workfare Program* (Washington: Government Printing Office, April 1984).

112.   This strategy was documented in the Cook County, Illinois, WIN program, producing 43,470 sanctions and disqualifications in a caseload of 101,000 recipients. The practice eventually provoked a lawsuit, curtailing the practice. See: Evelyn Z. Brodkin, "The Organization of Disputes: The Bureaucratic Construction of Welfare Rights and Wrongs," in S. Silbey and A. Sarat, eds., *Studies in Law, Politics, and Society* (Greenwich, Conn.: JAI Press, 1992), p. 69. On the use of sanctions in other WIN programs, see D. Friedlander *et al.*, 1987. On the misuse of sanctions in state general assistance programs, which operate free from federal regulation, see Michael Sosin, *Homelessness in Chicago*, Report to the Chicago Community Trust (Chicago: University of Chicago, School of Social Service Administration, 1988).

113.   Riccio *et al.*, pp. 25-29.

114.   For overviews of the Clinton administration's efforts to craft a welfare reform proposal, see Jason DeParle, "The Clinton Welfare Bill Begins Trek in Congress," *New York Times*, July 15, 1994, p. A1, Jeff Shear, "Pulling in Harness," *National Journal,* vol 26 (June 4, 1994) pp. 1286-1290, and David Whitman with Matthew

Cooper, "The End of Welfare — Sort of," *U.S. News and World Report*, June 20, 1994, pp. 28-37.

115.   Henry Aaron, *Why Is Welfare So Hard to Reform?* (Washington, D.C.: The Brookings Institution, 1973); Theodore Marmor and Martin Rein, "Reforming the 'Welfare Mess': The Fate of the Family Assistance Plan, 1969-1972," in Alan Sindler, ed., *Policy and Politics in America*, and Daniel Patrick Moynihan, *The Politics of a Guaranteed Income: The Nixon Administration and the Family Assistance Plan*, New York: Vintage, 1973.

116.   On the Carter initiative, see Laurence E. Lynn, Jr., and David def. Whitman, *The President as Policymaker: Jimmy Carter and Welfare Reform*, (Philadelphia: Temple University Press, 1981), and Christopher Leman, *The Collapse of Welfare Reform: Political Institutions, Policy and the Poor in Canada and the United States* (Cambridge, Mass.: MIT Press, 1980).

117.   Leman, *The Collapse of Welfare Reform*, p. 173.

118.   On the 1981 experience, see Edward D. Berkowitz, "Changing the Meaning of Welfare Reform," in John C. Weicher, ed., *Maintaining the Safety Net: Income Redistribution Programs in the Reagan Administration*, (Washington, D.C.: American Enterprise Institute, 1984), pp. 23-42.

119.   A brief history of the Family Support Act appears in Lawrence Mead, *The New Politics of Poverty*, New York: Basic Books, 1992, pp. 198-209. See also Erica L. Baum, "When the Witch Doctors Agree: The Family Support Act and Social Science Research." *Journal of Policy Analysis and Management*, vol. 10, no. 4 (Fall 1991) pp. 603-615.

120.   Charles Murray, "The Coming White Underclass," *Wall Street Journal*, October 29, 1993, p. A14.

121.   See Nancy Gibbs, "The Vicious Cycle," *Time*, June 20, 1994, p. 25, and Jason DeParle, "Abolishment of Welfare: An Idea Becomes a Cause," *New York Times*, April 22, 1994, p. A14.

122.   See Jason DeParle, "Proposal for Welfare Cutoff is Dividing Clinton Officials," *New York Times*, May 22, 1994, section 1, p. 20.

123.   See Eric Pianin, "Tenet of Clinton Welfare Plan Faces Test," *Washington Post*, May 20, 1994, p. A6

124.   See for example Jason DeParle, "Clinton Planners Facing A Quiet Fight on Welfare," *New York Times*, March 18, 1994, p. A18, and DeParle, "The Clinton Welfare Bill Begins Trek in Congress."

125.   See for example Tom Morgenthau et al, "The Orphanage," *Newsweek*, December 12, 1994, pp. 28-32.

126. For public opinion data and a discussion of G.O.P backpedaling on the orphanage issue, see Ronald Brownstein, "Clinton Sharply Attacks GOP's Orphanage Plan," *Los Angeles Times*, December 11, 1994, p. A1.

127. The exchange is reported in Nancy E. Roman, "Orphanages Fit into Clinton's Welfare Reform," *Washington Times*, January 11, 1995, p A1.

128. Ann Devroy, "House Republicans Get Talking Points," *Washington Post*, February 2, 1995, p. A9.

129. Elizabeth Shogren, "Key Republican Retreats on Welfare Reform," *Los Angeles Times*, December 2, 1994, p. A34.

130. See John Harwood, "GOP, Given Power by Voters Angry Over Welfare, Seeks a Compassionate Image in Welfare Debate," *Wall Street Journal*, March 22, 1995, p. A18.

131. See for example Jason DeParle, "Clinton Puzzle: How to Delay Welfare Reform Yet Seem to Pursue It," *New York Times*, January 5, 1994, p. A13.

132. On perverse incentives in the Clinton administration's welfare plan, see Mickey Kaus, "Tough Enough," *The New Republic*, April 25, 1994, pp. 22-25.

133. For details of the Budget Enforcement Act and its development, see James Edwin Kee and Scott V. Nystrom, "The 1990 Budget Package: Redefining the Debate," pp. 3-24, and Richard Doyle and Jerry McCaffery, "The Budget Enforcement Act of 1990: The Path to No-Fault Budgeting," pp. 25-40, in *Public Budgeting and Finance*, vol. 11 (Spring 1991).

134. On one short-lived administration revenue-raising initiative, see Jason DeParle, "Casinos Become Big Players in the Overhaul of Welfare," *New York Times*, May 9, 1994, p. A1. See also DeParle, "Paying for Welfare Promises Proves to Be the Hard Part," *New York Times*, February 22, 1994, p. A16, and DeParle, "A New Strategy for Welfare Overhaul," *New York Times*, April 21, 1994, p. D24.

135. Bob Woodward, *The Agenda: Inside the Clinton White House*, New York: Simon and Schuster, 1994, p. 132.

136. Woodward, *The Agenda*, p. 109. The first two promises were providing more jobs and health care reform.

137. Department of Health and Human Services, *Work and Responsibility Act: Detailed Summary*, June 1994.

138. For a critique of the block grant approach by a prominent conservative analyst, see Robert Rector, "Stringing Along," *National Review*, vol 47, no. 7, April 17, 1995, pp. 50-53.

139. See for example Lori Montgomery, "In Welfare Debate, Engler Is Both a Model and a Maverick," Detroit *Free Press*, January 20, 1995, p. 1A.

140. Jeffrey L. Katz, "Welfare Issue Finds Home on the Campaign Trail," *Congressional Quarterly Weekly Report*, vol. 52 (October 15, 1994) pp. 2956-2958.

141. As Rep. Jim Greenwood of Pennsylvania, put it, "I don't have to condition my support on perfection in the House vehicle . . . We all know the Senate will look at it closely." Jeffrey L. Katz, "GOP Moderates Central to Welfare Overhaul," *Congressional Quarterly Weekly Report*, March 18, 1995, p. 814.

142. Five Republicans voted against H.R. 4 on final passage, while 9 Democrats voted for it. Two of the five Republicans voting against it were Cuban Americans, and one opposed it because of concerns that it would increase abortion. See Robert Pear, "House Backs Bill Undoing Decades of Welfare Policy," *New York Times*, March 25, 1995, p. 1.

143. Bill McAllister, "Dole Criticizes House Plan; Teen Mothers' Welfare Cutoff Called Unlikely," *Washington Post*, January 23, 1995, p. A4.

144. On Dole, see Ronald Brownstein, "Dole Walks Fine Political Line in Bid for Presidency," *Los Angeles Times* [Washington edition] April 4, 1995, p. A6. On the conflict between Dole and Senate conservatives, see Hilary Stout, "After Early Success, GOP's Effort to Overhaul Welfare System May Be Derailed in the Senate," *Wall Street Journal*, July 6, 1995, p. A10, and Richard L. Berke, "Dole and Gramm Clash on Revising Laws on Welfare," *New York Times,* July 16, 1995, section 1, p. 1.

145. On the formula fights, see especially Jeffrey L. Katz, "Sunbelt Senators Revolt Over Welfare Formula," *Congressional Quarterly Weekly Report*, June 24, 1995, pp. 1842-1844.

146. Department of Health and Human Services and other departments, *The Work Opportunity Act of 1995, S. 1120: Senate Republican Leadership Plan; Impacts and Provisions; Children and Family Effects; State and Federal Program Effects*, August 7, 1995, section I, p. 10.

147. Jeffrey L. Katz, "Welfare Issue Finds Home on the Campaign Trail," p. 2958.

148. Hugh Heclo, "Poverty Politics," in Sheldon Danziger and Daniel Weinberg, eds., *Confronting Poverty: Prescriptions for Change*, (Russell Sage Foundation and Harvard University Press, 1994), pp. 396-437.

149. On Republican efforts, see in particular John Harwood, "GOP, Given Power by Angry Voters over Welfare, Seeks a Compassionate Image in Reform Debate," *Wall Street Journal*, March 22, 1995, p. A18; and Mona Charen, "High Ground on Welfare," *Washington Times*, March 22, 1995, p. A20.

150.   The quotation is from Representative Jan Meyers of Kansas in Ronald Brownstein, "Welfare Debate Puts Blame for Poverty Mainly on the Poor," *Los Angeles Times* (Washington edition), March 24, 1995, pp. A1, A8.

151.   David Binder, "Children Crusade against Proposed Republican Budget Cuts," *New York Times*, March 20, 1995, p. A13.

152.   The focus here is on examining modal positions of the public at large rather than examining differences among specific subgroups of the American population. For an analysis that stresses the views of particular subgroups, see Geoffrey Garin, Gary Molyneux, and Linda DiVall, *Public Attitudes toward Welfare Reform: A Summary of Key Research Findings*, Peter D. Hart Research Associates, American Viewpoint.

153.   For a more extensive presentation of recent trend data on welfare reform, see R. Kent Weaver, Robert Y. Shapiro, and Lawrence R. Jacobs, "Poll Trends: Welfare Reform," *Public Opinion Quarterly*, forthcoming.

154.   On the "dual clientele trap" in welfare reform, see chapter 5 in this volume and R. Kent Weaver, "Old Traps, New Twists: Why Welfare Is so Hard to Reform in 1994," *Brookings Review* (Summer 1994), pp. 18-21. See also Heclo's argument in "Poverty Politics" that Americans simultaneously feel a responsibility to help those who cannot help themselves, want to promote self-sufficiency, and seek to reduce poverty without explicitly embracing redistribution. The ambivalence theme in American attitudes toward social policy is addressed more generally in Jennifer L. Hochschild, *What's Fair: American Beliefs About Distributive Justice* (Cambridge, Mass.: Harvard University Press, 1981); and Stanley Feldman and John Zaller, "The Political Culture of Ambivalence: Ideological Responses to the Welfare State," *American Journal of Political Science*, vol. 36 (February 1992), pp. 268-307.

155.   Henry J. Kaiser Family Foundation, Kaiser-Harvard Program on the Public and Health-Social Policy, *Survey on Welfare Reform: Basic Values and Beliefs; Support for Policy Approaches; Knowledge about Key Programs*, January 1995.

156.   See Natalie Jaffe, "Attitudes toward Public Welfare Programs and Recipients in the United States," in Lester Salamon, *Welfare: The Elusive Consensus* (Praeger, 1978); Tom W. Smith, "That Which We Call Welfare by Any Other Name Would Be Sweeter: An Analysis of the Impact of Question Wording on Response Patterns," *Public Opinion Quarterly*, vol. 51 (1987), pp. 75-83; and Kenneth A. Rasinski, "The Effect of Question Wording on Public Support for Government Spending," *Public Opinion Quarterly,* vol. 53 (Fall 1989), pp. 388-94.

157.   On distinctions made by the public among recipients of income transfer programs, see Fax Lomax Cook, *Who Should Be Helped: Public Support for Social Services* (Beverly Hills: Sage, 1979), and Fay Lomax Cook and Edith J. Barrett, *Support for the American Welfare State: The Views of Congress and the Public* (New York: Columbia University Press, 1992).

158. Two percent of respondents thought that the welfare system worked very well, 14 percent fairly well. Comparable figures were 1 percent and 19 percent for the criminal justice system; 4 percent and 32 percent for the health care system; 5 percent and 34 percent for the education system; 3 percent and 36 percent for the tax system; and 9 percent and 49 percent for the Social Security system. Telephone poll of 1,020 respondents conducted between November 12 and 15, 1993, by Peter D. Hart Research Associates.

159. Five percent of respondents said some of both, 2 percent neither, and 1 percent not sure. These responses were very similar to those to an identically worded poll in January 1994: 19 percent "does more good than harm," 71 percent "does more harm than good," 5 percent some of both, 2 percent neither, and 1 percent not sure. Both polls were conducted by Hart/Teeter for NBC and the Wall Street Journal.

160. *Los Angeles Times* poll, Survey 334, National Issues, April 1994, question 75. In an April 1995 CBS/*New York Times* poll of 1,089 respondents, only 15 percent of respondents felt that "most people on welfare are using welfare for a short period of time and will get off it eventually," while 79 percent felt that "most people on welfare are so dependent on welfare that they will never get off it." Six percent had no opinion.

161. See Weaver, Shapiro, and Jacobs, "Poll Trends," for a detailed presentation of poll data. See also the discussion in Harvard/Kaiser, *Survey Shows "Two Faces" of Public Opinion on Welfare Reform*.

162. These observations about the effect on public opinion regarding welfare spending of the incumbent president's party are supported by the results of a time series (1973-1995, with three missing data years) regression equation predicting the percentage of the public saying that too much is being spent on welfare from two independent variables: the party of the president (dummy variable coded 0 for Republican and 1 for Democrat) and total federal and state spending in a fiscal year on AFDC benefits (in millions of constant 1992 dollars). The estimated equation,

$$\% \text{ saying "too much"} = 13.117(\text{Democrat}) + .002(\text{AFDC spending}) + 8.048$$
$$t = 5.130 \ (p = .0001) \quad t = 2.027 \ (p = .059)$$

N=20

$$\text{Adjusted R-square} = .66, \ F = 19.80 \ (p < .0001)$$
$$\text{Durbin-Watson} = 1.78,$$

indicates that the president's party and AFDC spending together explain two thirds of the variance over time in public opinion. Controlling for AFDC spending, the percent of the public saying too much is 13 percentage points higher during Democratic than Republican presidencies; and controlling for presidential party, this aggregate opinion increases two percentage points for every billion dollar increase in welfare spending increases. For a further discussion of the effect of government policies and other influences on public opinion, and the effect of public opinion on policymaking, see Robert H. Durr, "What Moves Policy Sentiment" *American Political Science Review*, 87 (March 1993) pp. 58-170; Benjamin Page and

Robert Y. Shapiro, *The Rational Public: Fifty Years of Trends in Americans' Policy Preferences* (Chicago: University of Chicago Press, 1992), and James A. Stimson, *Public Opinion in America: Moods, Swings and Cycles* (Boulder: Westview Press, 1991). On the determinants of public attitudes toward welfare spending, see James Kluegel, "Macro-Economic Problems, Beliefs about the Poor and Attitudes toward Welfare Spending," *Social Problems*, vol. 34 (February 1987), pp. 82-99, and Steven Michael Teles, *AFDC: The Politics of Dissensus*; Ph.D. dissertation, University of Virginia, January 1995, chap. 3.

163.   Six percent of those surveyed said that neither was a problem, and 5 percent were unsure. Peter D. Hart Research Associates-American Viewpoint, study 3805B, p. 4.

164.   See Stanley Feldman, "Structure and Consistency in Public Opinion: The Role of Core Beliefs and Values," *American Journal of Political Science*, vol. 32, pp. 416-438 for an examination of the role of beliefs and values in public opinion.

165.   When asked, "Of the people currently on welfare in the United States, how many would you say deserve to be receiving welfare benefits — nearly all, most but not all, about half, less than half, or almost none at all?," 4 percent of respondents said "nearly all"; 14 percent said "most, but not all," 42 percent said "about half," 32 percent said "less than half," 5 percent said "almost none at all," and 3 percent were not sure. Telephone poll of 1,020 respondents conducted between November 12 and 15, 1993, by Peter D. Hart Research Associates.

166.   See Heclo, "Poverty Politics." When asked in December 1994 whether "It is the responsibility of government to take care of people who can't take care of themselves," 65 percent agreed, 29 percent disagreed, and 6% didn't know. See Maureen Dowd, "Americans Like GOP Agenda But Split on How to Reach Goals," *New York Times*, December 15, 1994, p. A1. In another survey the same month, only 14 percent of respondents felt that government should have the primary responsibility for ensuring that nonworking low-income people have a minimum standard of living, with 26 percent believing that people themselves, their friends, and voluntary agencies should be responsible and 57 percent saying that responsibility should be shared. Most (71 percent) of those who believe that responsibility should be shared felt that government's obligation should be limited in duration, however. See Harvard/Kaiser, *Survey Shows "Two Faces" of Public Opinion on Welfare Reform*, table 23.

167.   When asked in December 1994, "Which is better for the children of unmarried mothers under 21 who have no income: to be placed in foster care or an orphanage or to remain with their mothers on welfare?," 20 percent said foster care/orphanage, 72 percent said remain with their mother, and 8 percent did not know. Dowd, "Americans Like GOP Agenda." When asked, somewhat differently, if they favored "a proposal that would end all welfare benefits for unmarried mothers and their children, even if it means that some of the children would have to be cared for in group homes or orphanages," 25 percent favored such a proposal, 66 percent opposed it, and 9 percent did not know or refused to answer. Harvard/Kaiser, *Survey on Welfare Reform*, table 22.

168.   In a poll by the Tarrance Group and Mellman, Lazarus and Lake in November 1993, respondents were asked "For each group on the following list of welfare recipients, please tell me whether you think time limits on collecting welfare, or A.F.D.C. (Aid to Families with Dependent Children) benefits should apply or should not apply." Time limits were favored by 64 percent of respondents for "single parents with drug or alcohol problems," as well as for "single parents with children under three years of age," and "single parents with children under one year of age." Agreement on time limits dropped to 57 percent for ""any family that cannot find a job where jobs are hard to find," and 38 percent for "any family where the parent has a significant physical or mental disability." But when asked in a poll by Peter D. Hart Research Associates/American Viewpoint the same month, "If there were a two-year limit on welfare benefits, would you favor a hard-and-fast cutoff for all able-bodied recipients after two years, or do you think the limit should be applied on a case-by-case basis?," only 19 percent favored a hard-and-fast cutoff, 79 percent favored a case-by-case basis, and 2 percent were not sure. When further asked in the same poll, "For each of the following cases, please tell me if the cutoff [without any job guarantee] should apply to this person after two years on welfare, or if an exception should be made in this case," making an exception was favored by 72 percent for "a mother with pre-school children," 59 percent for "someone who has worked for many years and is on welfare for the first time," 50 percent for "a teen mother who has not completed high school," 56 percent for "someone who lives in an area where the unemployment rate is more than 10 percent," 53 percent for "someone who is in a job-training program but still reads at the seventh-grade level," and 77 percent for "a mother on welfare who works part-time at a low-wage job."

169.   When asked the question, "Which is closer to your view: Welfare recipients should continue to get benefits as long as they work for them or after a year or two welfare recipients should stop receiving all benefits," in a December, 1994, CBS/*New York Times* survey, 71 percent chose getting benefits, 24 percent chose ending benefits, and 5 percent didn't know. Dowd, "Americans Like G.O.P. Agenda."

170.   When asked, "If government is going to cut off AFDC . . . or welfare benefits after a specific period of time and after it provides education, training, health benefits and child care to those families, should it. . . . " 10 percent of respondents chose "simply end the families' benefits, including Aid to Families with Dependent Children" 56 percent chose "make the parent or parents do community service work in exchange for welfare benefits" 25 percent favored "guarantee jobs to the parent or parents after they are cut off welfare"; 4 percent did not know; and 5 percent refused to answer. Harvard/Kaiser, *Survey on Welfare Reform*, table 18. These results are similar to those of a 1993 Hart/Teeter poll, which asked, "Which one of these two approaches to welfare reform would you say is better: 1) after two years, benefits would be ended for all able-bodied recipients, and the government would not provide any job; or 2) after two years, welfare recipients who have not found other employment would be required to work at a public service job?" Twelve percent of respondents chose cutting off benefits, 83 percent preferred requiring recipients to work at a public service job, and 2 percent each said both the same, neither, and not sure.

171.   Data for December 1994 are from Harvard/Kaiser, *Survey on Welfare Reform*. In an identically worded question in a November 1993 poll for *U.S. News and World Report*, 37 percent of respondents chose experiment at the state level, 43 percent, reform at the national level.

172.   Richard Morin, "Public Growing Wary of GOP Cuts," *Washington Post,* March 21, 1995, pp. A1, A6.

173.   The April CBS/*New York Times* survey stated: "Republicans in Congress have passed a number of changes to federal programs that serve the poor. Do you think the changes they have made go too far, do not go far enough, are about what is needed, or haven't you heard enough about these changes to say." "Too far" was chosen by 12 percent of respondents, 23 percent said "not far enough," 12 percent said "about what is needed," 48 percent had not heard enough to say, and 5 percent did not know or did not answer. The May results are from a Hart/Teeter poll for NBC and the *Wall Street Journal*.

174.   See John R. Zaller, *The Nature and Origins of Mass Opinion,* New York: Cambridge University Press, 1992.

175.   Kaus, "They Blew It," *New Republic*, December 5, 1994.

176.   Edward G. Carmines and James A. Stimson, *Issue Evolution: Race and the Transformation of American Politics* (Princeton: Princeton University Press, 1989).

Explanatory Notes for Tables and Figures in Chapter 6

The survey data reported here were compiled from searches of survey archives and published and unpublished sources, including the Roper Center for Public Opinion Research's on-line Public Opinion Location Library (POLL), *The Public Perspective: A Roper Center Review of Public Opinion and Polling*, the Inter-university Consortium for Political and Social Research (ICPSR, University of Michigan), data holdings of the Institute for Research in Social Science (IRSS, University of North Carolina), and the Times-Mirror Center for The People and The Press.

Abbreviations used for polling organizations and poll sponsors in Chapter 6 Tables

ABC/WP: ABC/Washington Post
HT: Hart/Teeter, and Peter D. Hart/American Viewpoint
LAT: Los Angeles Times
KRC for Harvard/Kaiser
NYT: Washington Times
TMLL for USNWR: Tarrance Group and Mellman, Lazarus and Lake for U.S. News and World
        Report
WSJ: Wall Street Journal
YP: Yankelovich Partners

Explanatory note for Table 6-2

All March questions on welfare are from the National Opinion Research Center. The question asks, "We are faced with many problems in this country, none of which can be solved easily or inexpensively. I'm going to name some of these problems, and for each one I'd like you to tell me whether you think we're spending too much money on it, too little money, or about the right amount. First, . . . are we spending too much, too little, or about the right amount on . . . welfare?" All data on "assistance for the poor" are from the same survey. No General Social Surveys were conducted in 1979, 1981, and 1992. Polls on welfare spending for November 1993 and April 1995 are from Hart/Teeter surveys (the latter for NBC and the Wall Street Journal) that asked "Do you think government is currently spending too little, about the right amount, or too much on . . . people on welfare." The January 1995 survey asked "Now I am going to read some areas of government spending, and for each one, tell me if you think the government should spend less in this area, spend more in this area, or spend about the same as it does now . . . welfare." The November 1993 data on spending for poor children is from a Hart poll that asked, "Do you think government is currently spending too little, about the right amount, or too much on . . . poor children?" The December 1994 poll on this topic is from a CBS/New York Times poll that asked, "Do you think government spending on programs for poor children should be increased, decreased, or kept about the same?"

Explanatory note for Figure 6-1

Data in this figure are derived from multiple polls using slightly different wordings. Data for March 1982 are from a CBS/New York Times Poll asking "In your opinion, what is more often to blame if people are poor — lack of effort on their own part, or circumstances beyond their control?" Data for December 1984, July 1988 and August 1989 are from a Gallup poll asking "In your opinion, which is more often to blame if a person is poor — lack of effort on his own part, or circumstances beyond his control?" Data for May 1990 are from a Gallup poll asking "Just your opinion: which is more often to blame if a person is poor — lack of effort on his or her own part, or circumstances beyond his or her control?" Data for December 1990 are from a New York Times poll and for December 1994 from a CBS/New York Times poll asking "In your opinion, what is more to blame when people are poor — lack of effort on their own part, or circumstances beyond their control?" Data for February 1992 are from a Los Angeles Times poll asking "In your opinion, which is more often to blame if a person is poor — lack of effort on their own part, or circumstances beyond their control?" Data for November 1993 are from a Hart Teeter poll asking "In your opinion, which is the bigger cause of poverty today — people not doing enough to help themselves out of poverty, or circumstances beyond people's control that cause them to be poor?"; data for April 1995 are also from a Hart Teeter poll with wording identical to the earlier one except for asking about the " . . . bigger cause of poverty and people being poor today . . . " For a presentation of the data, see R. Kent Weaver, Robert Y. Shapiro and Lawrence Jacobs, "Poll Trends: Welfare Reform, *Public Opinion Quarterly*, forthcoming.

Explanatory note for Figure 6-2

Data in this figure are derived from multiple polls using slightly different wordings. Where multiple polls were available for a single month, results of the polls were averaged. Data for January 1993 are from a Greenberg/Lake poll asking, "I would like to read you a list of issues that some people from this part of the country have said are important for the federal government to deal with. Please listen as I read the list and tell me, for each one, whether you think — 1) President Clinton or 2) the Republicans in Congress — could do a better job dealing with this issue . . . Reforming the welfare system." Data for January 1994 are from a Blum and Weprin poll for NBC News asking "Who do you think would do the best job reforming the welfare system — President (Bill) Clinton or the Republicans in Congress?" Data for April 1994 and October 1994 are from a Los Angeles Times poll asking "Who do you think can do a better job of reforming the welfare system: President (Bill) Clinton or the Republicans in Congress?" Data for August 1994 and April 1995 are from a Tarrance Group and Mellman and Lake poll asking "Now I would like to read you a list of issues that some people from this part of the country have said are important for the federal government to deal with. Please tell me, for each one, whether you have more confidence in Bill Clinton and the Democrats in Congress or the Republicans in Congress to deal with this issue . . . Reforming the welfare system." Data for November 1994 and January 1995 are from a Hart/Teeter poll for the Wall Street Journal and NBC asking "For each of the following issues, please tell me if you think that President (Bill) Clinton or the Republicans in Congress generally will have the better approach to this issue, or if there will not be much difference. Who do you think will have a better approach to . . . welfare reform — President Clinton or the Republicans in Congress, or do you think there won't be much difference on this issue." Data for December 1994 are from two CBS/New York Times poll asking "Who do you think would make better decisions about reforming the welfare system — the Republicans in Congress or (President) Bill Clinton?" and "Who do you think would be more likely to make decisions about reforming the welfare system that are fair to all Americans — the Republicans in Congress or

(President) Bill Clinton?" and a third poll by Princeton Survey Research Associates for Newsweek asking "As I read off some statements, tell me whether you think each applies more to (President) Bill Clinton or more to Republican leaders in Congress. How about . . . has better ideas for reforming the welfare system." Data for February 1995 are from a similar PSRA survey. Data for January 1995 and April 1995 are from a CBS/New York Times poll asking "Who do you think has better ideas about reforming the welfare system: President Clinton, or the Republicans in Congress?" Data for March 1995 and July 1995 are from an ABC/Washington Post poll asking "For each specific issue I name, please tell me who you trust to do a better job handling that issue — (Bill) Clinton or the Republicans in Congress." For a presentation of the data, see R. Kent Weaver, Robert Y. Shapiro and Lawrence Jacobs, "Poll Trends: Welfare Reform, *Public Opinion Quarterly*, forthcoming.